Love Stories with My Beloved

Love Stories with My Beloved

Jennifer K. Davis

CROSSBOOKS
PUBLISHING

CrossBooks™
A Division of LifeWay
1663 Liberty Drive
Bloomington, IN 47403
www.crossbooks.com
Phone: 1-866-879-0502

First published by CrossBooks 10/18/2011

ISBN: 978-1-4627-0667-9 (sc)
ISBN: 978-1-4627-1057-7 (e)
ISBN: 978-1-4627-1137-6 (hc)

Printed in the United States of America

Edited by Brittany Lowe, Jennifer Davis, Katy Chisholm, Kendra Houliston, Kim Davis; Front Cover picture by Jenae Tankersley; Inside final picture by Colin Lokken

This book is printed on acid-free paper.

To my Love, You have my heart. You pursued
me to life. All I have is Yours.
And to my love. Whoever you are. Wherever you are. Keep
waiting. I promise I am coming. All my love. ~Yours

Table of Contents

The Beginning
Introduction

In order for you to truly understand the concept of this book, I need to explain a few things first. This is not a novel, nor is it another self-help book. *Love Stories with My Beloved* is simply a set of visions, dreams, and stories designed to assist you and me as we walk through this journey of exploring what it means to be the beloved and bride of Christ. During my sophomore year in college, the Lord gave me a vision of my wedding day with Him. Since that moment, He has been showing me His desire to walk with me not only as Savior, Father, Healer, Friend, Protector, etc but as Husband. The story of the wedding day did not actually happen, but rather was a vision given to me and later analyzed for deep revelation. However, some of the love stories written in these pages were birthed from actual encounters between the Lord and myself.

I hope it is okay if I embark with you on this journey to becoming beloved. It is my heart's desire that you not only read straight through as if this is just another book, but rather I encourage you to truly listen as the Holy Spirit speaks to your heart. At the end of each section you will find places to journal and create your own moments with Jesus as Husband. Please do not miss those precious opportunities with the Lord.

I make a promise to you now to be completely open and honest with you about the things the Lord spoke to me through these moments. Some of them could seem a little embarrassing; however understanding my true identity in Him, I am able to move past the pride and be vulnerable with you. I challenge you, as I am being open and honest with you, will you do the same with the Lord?

Use the journal sections to really pin down in your heart what He is saying to you. I promise you will not regret it. At the end of this journey you will be able to look back and read in your handwriting, the victory and beautiful romance between you and Jesus.

♥

Sometimes I think as women we desire so much to be pursued, loved, cherished, and desired by our husbands, boyfriends, or friends that we forget our wonderful Savior longs to fill every void in our hearts. I find it interesting the phenomenon that started quite a few years ago about staying sexually pure until marriage and reserving a special place in our heart for our future husband. Now do not get me wrong, I am certainly an advocate for remaining sexually pure until marriage, and I am definitely a believer in marriage.

However, there are two things wrong with this idea. One is it completely ignores the idea of staying emotionally, as well as, physically pure before marriage. Another problem is it also alludes to the idea that it is acceptable to God that we save part of our heart for the man we will marry. Am I not mistaken that the Word of God says we are to love the Lord our God with ALL our heart? Maybe that is a little too much for the introduction. Let us just start from the beginning of my journey and see where we end up at the conclusion of our time together.

Section 1: The Wedding Day
Becoming the Bride

The Wedding Day

There I was, standing in the middle of a field, in a torn, dirty, what used to be white dress. There was mud caked along the bottom of my dress and rips down the side, as if it had been pulled at and worn too long. How did I get here? Something was not right. I was standing in that field filled with complete fear: fear of the unknown, fear of failure, and fear of rejection.

As I was standing alone in the field, I knew something was wrong, but I could not quite put my finger on what it was. My eyes were cast down, gazing at the rags draped across my body, as I pondered how I ended up there in that giant field. As I was lost in my thoughts and fears, I suddenly caught a glimpse of movement out of the corner of my eye. Awakened back to reality, I had this sudden feeling as if I were not alone. Something began to stir into motion, and I could hear rustling in the distance as I became slightly aware of something moving closer. As I slowly lifted my eyes upwards, I realized I was most certainly not alone.

Out in the distance there were what appeared to be dozens and dozens of men. As my eyes glanced around, I noticed the dreary weather settling across the pasture. Gray clouds were creeping into the gloomy sky, and there was a line of men moving my direction. It looked like a battle scene straight from a war movie. The men continued coming my direction, but not running as if they were going to chase me. Instead, it was as if these men were walls closing in around me. As they surrounded me I felt the unexplainable need to run. Not only a need but also a desire to run away. But I was so scared. The weight of all of my fears oppressed me until I felt frozen and unable to move.

Then finding a surge of unexplainable strength, I found myself running. I started off slow, but in no time at all I began to pick up the

3

pace. I had no idea I could move this quickly; it was as if I was given a super natural power to run. My breathing remained steady as my body began to feel lighter and lighter with each stride I took. It was almost as if I received more strength with each step. After a few moments of running, I noticed that I was entering into a small, deserted looking town. I remember thinking disappointedly that something special must have been going on. Maybe in the next town over there was a huge event I did not know about, which is where all the people were.

As I sprinted further into the town, I found myself running past a building with a tall steeple on the top. The building was a beautiful old structure filled with character and charm. I was drawn to the place but felt I must keep running. I jogged to the back of the building and began navigating down a deserted and rummage-filled alley. Climbing over boxes and squeezing past crates, my eyes glanced upon things familiar. In the midst of the rummage were pieces of my past. Scraps of papers with painful words that had been spoken to me overflowed the boxes. Torn pictures of hard and lonely places I had been peeked through the holes in the crates.

Quickly remembering why I had turned the corner and into the alley, I began to search for an escape. Frantically looking around I noticed there was a set of steps leading up to an old door, and I knew at any moment my trackers would come bounding around the corner. I knew my only way out was either to go up those steps and through that old door, or continue running into an eventual dead end. The door I saw was not a huge door, but it certainly was a door that served a purpose. I reached for the wooden, aged doorknob, which had been worn down from being opened so many times. The door was heavier than I expected, and it took a little effort to open. But as I started to pull it, the door practically swung itself wide open, banging against the wall as it did so.

Unsure of what was inside, I looked up and realized at that moment I had just interrupted the beginning of a wedding. The people in the audience turned and looked at me. Their reaction was quite surprising to me, because they were not upset or annoyed that I had rudely disrupted their event. Instead, the people smiled at me as if something was happening of which I was unaware. In a split second, comprehension dawns. This was not just anyone's wedding...it was mine.

Something within that very moment began to feel different. I looked down and clothing me now was no longer dirt and rags, but the most beautiful dress a girl could ever dream of wearing. It was perfectly white, fit me like a glove, and had the perfect amount of class and elegance, with a sparkle of royalty. "Wait a minute," I thought to myself, "this is where the whole town was... at my wedding? But who had called them, who had summoned the people?" As this all began to stir within my mind, the audience stood, the music began, and I now had the decision to take the first step down the aisle. I knew if I went back out those doors, there was nothing awaiting me but fear and disappointment. But who was this man I was marrying?

It was then that I saw him. The most beautiful man I had ever laid my eyes on. He was gazing at me in a way any girl would only dream about. I remember in an instant falling devotedly in love again. This man was no stranger; he was my love, my heart's desire. With just one look into his eyes, it all began to come back to me, and there was nowhere else I would rather be but to be walking towards him.

♥

Let us rewind a little bit. You see I had known from the moment I met him years ago that he was the one for me. From the very first day he romanced me, blessed me, and loved me. The second he introduced himself to me, I somehow felt life could not be complete without him. He had asked for my hand in marriage, and since I had met him, I could not imagine living without him. So I quickly gave my answer, "Yes!" The way he comforted me when I was afraid, the way he built me up when I felt discouraged, these were all things no other man had been able to demonstrate to me. I was in love.

However, throughout our relationship, even though he was so good to me, there would be times I would want to give up on us. Difficult situations and my own insecurities would cause me to question, could this love really be true? The world that surrounded me taught me that perfect love did not exist. There was no way a man could love me perfectly.

The moment I would take my eyes off him, I remembered all of the things I had done and how unworthy I felt of his affection. Every once in awhile, when my eyes left his gaze I would leave. I would try to search for other things that could captivate my heart the way he did. At least if I could find something else to distract me from how perfect he was and how undeserving I was, it would be easier.

However, nothing ever fulfilled me quite like he did. In fact, nothing ever came close. Every time I turned away from him or found my eyes focusing on another man, he was still there. I could see the pain in his eyes when I would leave him for something else, but there was a part of me that just wanted to leave anyway. Deep down I knew I could find no one better, no one willing to love me the way he did in spite of all my flaws. Yet even still, I would leave him anyway. You see he had asked for my hand in marriage, and I had said yes. Nevertheless there were these moments when I would forget that he was all I needed and even all I wanted.

It all came flooding back to me. The period of time leading up to the wedding I had decided to leave again and enter into a season of wandering. He continued to pursue me and tried demonstrating to me in so many ways his love for me. All I had to do was walk down the aisle to him. My love would try to persuade me and remind me that he was all I needed, but he knew I was going to walk away, despite his faithfulness. So with sadness, my love let go of my hand, told me he would be waiting for me at the altar, and would never stop loving me. He whispered in my ear right before I left, "There is nothing you will ever do that will keep my whole heart from being yours. I'll be waiting."

I thought, "I am engaged to him, I have already said yes to him, but I need some time before the wedding to make sure this is the right decision." I justified within myself that I had already said yes, this season was just for me. Hence, I decided to go, to wander into the wilderness. I do not even know why I did it really: selfishness, insecurity, and fear. Those were the only things I could determine that were driving this disaster. So I put on the handmade wedding dress I had spent so long creating and left. It was not that I planned to never return and marry him. There was just this fear of commitment in me. The question I asked myself was "Am I really ready to marry him?"

In this season of wandering, all I could seem to do was walk. I would walk for miles and miles just thinking. It would rain, storms would come, and still I would wander, never stopping to seek shelter or wipe off the water from the rain. I would trek around in the mud asking myself, "Am I really worthy to be loved by him? Could I really please such an incredible man? Would I be a good wife to him?" There would even be times that I would look at another man and find a desire in me to be with him. I would ponder on the kind of relationship this other man could offer me, but it always came up short to what my true love could offer. Then one day, after way too long wandering and way too many men falling short, I found myself scared in the field and then well… about to take the first step down the aisle.

♥

Back to that first step down the aisle. The pursuit of my love is so important to this story. If it had not been for his consistent pursuit of me, I would never have taken that first step. However in that moment, because I knew that it was him who had called me beloved, who had promised to love and cherish me forever, and it was him that I found my complete purpose for living, I could now take that first step.

And so I did. I placed one foot in front of the other and began to walk down the aisle towards him. In what seemed like an instant, I was there at the end of the aisle, standing at the front of the altar, staring into my beloved's face. If only I could adequately describe the next few events, I am sure I would have every single one of you in tears and completely in love with this man.

In the moment every girl dreams about, the time the man you love professes his enduring love to you in front of all the people you care for, there is a sense of pride and ownership that comes over you. "This is mine," you think, "he is mine." My life leading up to this point, had all been to be here, standing at that altar saying yes. Nothing and no one in that instant compares to the love for the man you are staring at. It is as if you loose yourself in his eyes. The butterflies, the excitement, the peace, so many emotions for one decision…to say "I do."

What happened next in the story is precious. I remember hearing my father's voice. You see my father was going to be marrying us that day. When my father began the ceremony, his voice did not distract me from my love standing in front of me or the moment we were experiencing. Instead his voice drew me nearer, and brought fullness and completion to the devotion between me and my love.

I remember my father giving a charge to my love. This was the most significant event throughout the whole ceremony. My father told him, "You are to care for her more than you care for yourself. You will sacrifice everything you have, just so she can wake up and have one more day to be my daughter, to be your wife, to be the woman I have desired for her to be. You are to provide for her, to meet her needs. There are times she will run, there are times she will hurt you, there are times she will not want to be with you. Love her anyway. You will love her with a perfect love, yet she will often forget it. You will often protect her when she does not even realize she needs protection. You will pursue her for the rest of her days. You are to die for her so that she may live."

Not fully able to comprehend everything my father just said, I stood there in awe. Without hesitation, my love said "With pleasure."

Now it was my turn. My father turned to me. Within my father's gaze I see complete joy, peace, and confidence in my decision. With a loving voice he told me, "You, my daughter, *honor him*. You will be cared for, provided for, unalterably loved. You will often run from this, but your love will always remain, waiting for your return, ready to forgive. You will be protected, desired, found worthy, and pursued all the days of your life. You need only say, 'I do.'"

And because of my father's confidence and the man standing before me, I was able and more than willing to whisper my answer…"I do."

♥

There is still more to the ceremony, but in honor of suspense the rest will come in the last section of the book. So prepare yourself, because with a love this good, he never ceases to amaze.

THE BREAKDOWN

And no, when I say breakdown I do not mean an emotional moment where I lose all control and cry for days. You see there is such significance to this story. Some of you may still think this is a love story about my earthly husband and me. However, this is no typical man. This Love in which I spoke of has a name, and he is available for each one of us. His name is Jesus.

Each part of this story has such a unique meaning and purpose. This section of the book is meant to breakdown each detail of the story and discover the spiritual truth behind this journey. Let us jump right in from the beginning. Please remember as I mentioned in the introduction, these are just my interpretations. They are meant to encourage you to see things you might not have considered before. If you relate to them then great, if not, ask the Holy Spirit for your own interpretation. Remember to journal your thoughts so you can have a memoir of your journey to becoming beloved.

The field and the men

The field was my place of recognition. Something in my life was just not right. I had been blinded in a way, or had my eyes downward for so long I could not see how lost in myself I had become. For many of us this looks in a practical sense like those times in our lives where we are utterly helpless, almost defeated. We end up here when we forget the relationship and role we have been called to live by our Father God.

It is important that I stop here for a moment. I want to be perfectly clear what I am speaking about. For many people, the field represents the place in their life right before salvation. However, for others (myself included) who are already believers, this could be a spot you have found yourself in quite often. Either way it is a type of wandering experience. As believers, we often forget our role and relationship with Jesus and go into seasons of wandering, which we will discuss more in detail later. But for the point of this story, this is one of those wandering seasons.

Remember how I mentioned the dark clouds and gloomy sky? Even the atmosphere and the weather seem threatening in moments of wandering. These things can represent our feelings during these times. Often in seasons of wandering, we can begin to feel depressed, discouraged, or frustrated. Also during these times, we can feel so alone, but sooner or later we realize we are not. We need to identify these feelings for what they are, which are side effects to our wandering. Depression, loneliness, and frustration are not feelings we have when we are in right fellowship with the Lord.

Realizing the identity of these men who appeared in this field is crucial to experience freedom from their gripping hold in our lives.

At first glance, when you begin to notice you are not alone and there are in fact dozens of men in front of you, the men appear to take on characteristics of past men you have been involved with. Your involvement with these men could have been physical or emotional relationships you entered at some point in our life. In fact they look so much like those men from a distance that you would never think otherwise, unless they got closer.

However, this is where most of us would stop analyzing. Okay, so we realize we have given ourselves away and we need to repent, turn from our sin, forgive the men who have hurt us, and move on. But it is so much more than that! I said at first glance they appear to be men from your past. However, when you really begin to look closely at them, they are not solely those men. Instead, they are actually little images of yourself that you invested into each particular man.

Something I had to realize during this stage was that God was not only trying to get me to break an emotional tie with another person, but also with the part of myself that I had given them. I had developed ideas of who I should be with each man. Little false identities and bondages of insecurity were attached to each person. Those bondages birthed within me anger and in some circumstances bitterness. For each different man, there was a piece of false identity that I had put on myself that God had never designed for me to wear.

What is so crucial about this realization is that you not only forgive these men, but that you also forgive yourself. The real freedom comes when you learn to remove the false identities and insecurities and walk in forgiveness in your true identity. You are not bound by what you think you should be or the way you think you should act. You are not bound by the attitudes and characteristics you once wore for the approval of man. You are free to be you!

Now take a moment. Seriously, put the book down for the day. Allow the Lord to let this settle within you. Identify the people in your life you have given part of yourself to. Forgive those things that were done and said that hurt you. Do not stop there though. Go deeper. Forgive yourself. Remove the false identity, and ask the Lord to begin to show you exactly who He created you to be. Make a list of the characteristics you feel the Lord designed for you. Who are you in His eyes?

_____

_____

_____

_____

_____

The feelings and the running

So let's address the feelings associated with this season of wandering. This is by no means an exhaustive list but the ones I identified with. While we have already mentioned a few (depression, frustration, etc.) the main root to all of these feelings is fear, but fear manifests itself in specific ways. For me those fears were fear of failure, fear of rejection, and fear of the unknown.

There I was standing in the field about to be chased down by dozens of men, and I stood there too afraid to move. An unhealthy fear is like a weight of bondage and holds us down, which is exactly why the fears felt crippling in that moment. This is so often what our fear does. It paralyzes us in a place where we are weak and vulnerable. When I was feeling threatened, I was in a state of vulnerability to all of the elements surrounding me. The key here however, was the impulse I had to run. This is where the escape started. Right there, in the thought to get away. Even though I did not know how, or even if I could, nonetheless, there was the desire to run.

I truly believe that God waits for us to simply desire to get away, and He begins to move us supernaturally in His direction. What I find so interesting is that even though I was too afraid to move, He gave me the strength to take the first step, because he knew the desire of my heart. With each step, I gained more confidence and less fear, for perfect love casts out fear (1 John 4:18). Then He honored each step with another, to where I was not only jogging but running. And not only was I running but He put me in the right direction, so that when I ran I would be headed towards safety and deliverance.

Be careful to note here, God does not come in and overtake our bodies to get us to move. He gives us a choice. When He sees the pure desire of our heart to get out of our messes, He enables our escape. But I had to choose to take those first steps. He helped me when I was weak, but I ultimately had to decide to move. Where are you now? Is there anything holding you back? What are your fears?

_____

_____

_____

_____

_____

The town and the alley

Once I got into the town after all of my running do you remember what I found? Nothing. I had finally left the season of wandering and the first place I came to seemed deserted. I found no one there to help me or offer me shelter. At first, it can often feel this way when we come out of a wandering period, and the temptation is to give up right then and there. When no one else seems to understand where we are coming from or what we have been through, we want to throw in the towel. However, what I did not realize was that He was already working things out for me. I just had to keep moving.

Coming to the alley is a very hard place to arrive and often comes at a very difficult time. The timing and situation to us looks like the end. We are exhausted from running, then find ourselves trapped in a passage with no way out. If we had not wanted to already, at that moment we really want to quit. Not only that, but in the alley I began to find pictures which held snapshots of hurtful and lonely times of my past. So when I was already down, more reminders of my life's tragedies reared their ugly face.

The glorious thing about this picture is what looks like the end to me, is really the final moments right before the biggest breakthrough of my life. I often ask the Lord why I had to see those pictures and memories right before I opened the door and walked inside. His response to me is, "Why did you focus so much on the pictures and memories instead of the fact that they were all boxed up and out by the trash? What you did not know is that once you walked through that door the garbage man was coming and every piece of filth and trash from your life was about to be removed and burned for all of eternity."

So my encouragement to you in this is: Are you still focusing on the trash and filth instead of the fact that God has boxed it up and wants to throw it away? Every time you think about those boxes, you are not allowing the Lord to throw them away as He intended. What are your boxes of garbage? Leave them in the alley today once and for all, and remember the trash man is coming to remove the garbage. Also, remember if you are in that alleyway, breakthrough is moments away.

_____

_____

_____

_____

_____

The door, the dress, and the guest list

Moment by moment, throughout the breakdown of this story, I realize just how present the Lord was with me through every step of my return. When I went to open the door, it was very heavy. I had to use effort and intentionality to open it. However, as soon as I began to tug on the door, it flung completely open alerting everyone of my arrival. Just as God had provided me the strength to run, I had to take the first step, God helped me open the door, but I had to first pull on the handle.

But why though did it have to be so hard to return? Why did it feel like throughout every step of my return process I came to such difficult moments? While this might not be exactly what we want to hear in times like this, the answer I believe is that our decisions have consequences. We are held accountable for what we know. I already knew Jesus as my Savior, but I decided to leave anyway. For that reason, my journey back was difficult, but I believe God is all about honoring obedience. Even when we have been disobedient, He simply waits for us to make that first step or slightly pull on that handle, and He will do the rest. Where sin abounds, His grace abounds much more (Romans 5:20). I am telling you, He is so faithful. He is for us not against us (Romans 8:31).

Once I stood inside the building the transformation instantaneously began. For instance, my dress had been restored. He had taken my rags and turned them into a richly and perfectly created masterpiece. It had been tailor designed to fit me. God has a way of knowing what attire looks best on us. (And no, I do not merely mean physically!) There was no more dirt or imperfections on me. All of the shame and filth from my past had been left outside that door. This was no ordinary wedding dress nor was this an ordinary wedding. I mentioned my dress had the sparkle of royalty. What I had forgotten until that moment was the man I had said yes to marry was no ordinary man. Instead He was a prince, for His father was the King.

So where were the townspeople? Well, they had been summoned to a royal wedding of course! Just as in the world today, when there is royal wedding, everyday activities seem to cease and all eyes are on the royal couple. During this wedding in particular, the King had called all the people to come and partake in the uniting of His beloved son and His bride.

Right before I took that first step down the aisle, I was able to see the faces of those awaiting my arrival. As I looked around, I saw the faces of my family, the ones alive today as well as the ones who had passed away. The family members present at the ceremony were those who had labored in prayer for me all throughout my life. I saw friends who had encouraged me to stay strong, to always come back to my first love. Leaders and pastors from my past and present were also among the crowd. They watched me and smiled, so proud of this very moment. Their presence during this moment meant so much to me. My Love must have known how I would have desired their company during this glorious ceremony. Every detail was perfectly planned and completed for me.

Thank Him for His perfect plan. Even though it does not always seem perfect at the time, He is working all things for your good (Romans 8:28). Who are the attendees of your wedding? Take a moment and really ponder on those people in your life that helped you get to this point of marriage to the Prince of your hearts. Take some time and pray for those loved ones who are not at the ceremony. Those who still need to meet Jesus and say yes to His proposal. When you realize just how beautifully crafted those people are into your life, you will fall more in love with the One who created that design.

_____

_____

_____

_____

_____

The rewind and the introduction

Before we continue on with the ceremony, there are still a few details of the story that need to be explained. We must go back to the moment I met him. As I previously mentioned, this was a wonderful encounter. Meeting my Love was like nothing I had ever experienced before. I very quickly said yes to His hand in marriage.

I want to give a prelude to this next discussion. Everyone's picture of these next few moments will be different. I am merely explaining my own interpretation on my walk with the Lord. So read mine, but really stop to think about your journey as well.

When I met the Lord, it was an incredible experience and at a very innocent moment in my life. However, for some of you, meeting Jesus may have come at a very difficult point in life. Hard things were occurring all around you and your circumstances prepared your heart for the ultimate surrender. It does not matter the circumstance, what matters is that your answer was yes.

The moment I said yes to marry Him, I believe, represents my moment of salvation. So many people have met Jesus, know who He is, but have not said yes to His call. It is very easy to get distracted here and begin to analyze if the moment of salvation is here or when you say "I do" at the altar. As I said it could look different for many, this is just my revelation for the story.

So again, what is your introduction moment with the Lord and what was it like when you said yes to His proposal? I am serious; write the testimony of your salvation now. It is part of your love story. Some of you have been reading this book and are thoroughly confused until this point. You did not understand that our walk with God is about a relationship not just knowledge. If you have never given your heart to the Lord and said yes to His call, I encourage you to stop now, go to the back of the book and pray the prayer of salvation. (See Appendix II) He longs to enter into a loving, romantic relationship with you.

_____

_____

_____

_____

_____

The prelude to the season of wandering

Once we accept Jesus as our Savior, our chief danger is believing our enemies lies, which have been growing since the beginning of creation. Before any season of wandering, there is usually a lie heard then believed. Belief is the time the lie becomes venomous to us. To hear a lie or even think of one is not our struggle. Our struggle occurs when that thought becomes a belief. Our beliefs are what drive us to make our decisions.

This is the part where I become extremely vulnerable and explain the lies I myself would constantly believe. The idea of my value and worth would be an ever-present thought in mind. I would begin to compare myself with others around me and worse still, to an idea of who I thought I should be. It became a pattern of mine to take my eyes off of my Love and look at all my imperfections, the places in my life I lacked perfection.

I did this so much that these thoughts eventually became my beliefs. I was not good enough. I was not worthy enough. Eventually, the lies even led me to question if I was really satisfied with Jesus. Was He really all I wanted? Did He satisfy my every longing? …Wait, am I being too honest right now?

These questions and doubts of my identity would constantly bombard me until it was just easier to believe in the lies. Therefore, although belief is what eventually harms us, it all begins with the thought of a lie. The Word says whatever is true, right, pure, etc. meditate on these things (Philippians 4:18). What if when those lies first came to my mind, I had just taken a few minutes to speak the truth of God's Word over my life, instead of dwelling on (and eventually digesting) the lie? I imagine that those seasons of wandering would have been non-existent.

When our hearts and minds are focused on Him and His truth, it is impossible to be deceived by a lie. His Word tells me I am valued, loved, cherished, and found worthy through His eyes. But so often my focus shifts, and I am deceived into submitting to the trap of the lies.

If I can be even more honest with you, often I am still faced with doubts of my value. However, now I know that it is my choice to *believe* the lie or *change* the lie suggested by the enemy into a truth written and declared by God.

What are the lies you often believe that draw you away from the Lord? What has been spoken over you so many times, either by yourself or others that you have come to believe as truth? Look for evidence of the lie that would make it true. I guarantee there is none. That is how we know they are lies. There was no legitimate evidence to my unworthiness or imperfections. They had all been covered by the blood of Jesus. In fact, when I really look closely, what I had thought was truth (my unworthiness and little value) were actually the fabricated lies of

the enemy. I was exactly opposite of the lie which had defined me. I was
worthy, and I was greatly valued.

The season of wandering

Unfortunately, we have all been here at some point or another. It is imperative to note that a season of wandering is not the same as a season in the wilderness. A season of wandering is a choice we make; a time in the wilderness is a place the Lord will often take us. (More on that later.)

Do you remember how after my engagement I walked away from my Beloved for a season of independence? If you recall, my Love did not desire for me to leave. In fact, He did everything He could to ask me to stay. It was my decision to leave. I chose to believe the lies and distance myself from my Love.

Out of my selfishness and fear, I left. The thought I had, not to be easily missed, was that I was already engaged. I had already said yes to marry him. In my mind, this justified my abandonment. There was a lack of commitment in me that I would not fully discover until the wedding day. So many believers are more interested in fire insurance (freedom from hell, a.k.a. salvation) and not in the abundant life guarantee through total commitment.

The wandering is such a lonely and confusing place. We become completely vulnerable to the elements; there is little protection from the storms. Our desire for completion and fulfillment in the season of wandering will often lead us to counterfeit solutions.

Leaving can be a huge decision and often contemplated beforehand.

The quiet yet dramatic exit of uncertainty, such as this one was for me. Or it can take the form of a dramatically blatant desertion or a subtle drifting as little decisions here and there distract your attention from Jesus. For some, the season stems from a desire for complete rebellion where huge decisions are intentionally made in contradiction to God's Word. I am convinced that no matter how the season comes, they all look the same to the Lord. They are all moments lacking intimacy and unity with Him, two things He so greatly desires.

Although the effects of wandering (lack of intimacy and unity) are the same, the outcomes of our return vary from person to person. Sometimes it is with the slightest turn of our head that we are back into fellowship with Him. Other times it takes being chased by men, running through a field and deserted town, and stumbling through a rummage-filled alley to find ourselves back in His presence. God lovingly corrects each one of His children specifically to their needs (Proverbs 13:24).

One more thing to discuss before we get back to the ceremony is the handmade wedding dress. As clothing here represents identity, it is no wonder that my flimsy attempt fell apart under the pressure of the storms. Often we spend so much time creating our own garments, we miss out on the ones He desires to clothe us in. Imagine if I had allowed Him sooner to clothe me in the beautiful gown He had created. I wonder if His garments (His identity) would have protected me from my season of wandering. And why did He create such a beautiful garment? I mean the wedding dress is only worn for a day. Eventually I would become the wife and not just the engaged bride. But He is so much more purposeful than that.

He would allow me to wear the dress every single day for the rest of eternity. He knew the dress would serve as a reminder of my decision and that He would always carry me as His bride and love me the same as He did on my wedding day. Oh, I would become His wife, of course, but I would remember that nothing I could do or say would allow me to earn more of His love. It was all mine right then. Every ounce of His love was available for me that day. My joy as His wife would be realizing each day the depths of His love. So please make a special note that we are always the bride. The pivotal point we need to be made aware of is there is a difference between the engaged bride and the married bride.

Okay so you know the drill. What do your season of wanderings 'ow do you feel during those seasons of wandering? Does ade garment unravel? How do you react to the exposure? w Him to clothe you in masterpiece that will last forever?

_____

_____

_____

_____

_____

The ceremony and saying "I Do"

Finally, the time had come. I took my first steps toward becoming the wife of my Beloved. The only reason I was able to take those steps was because I realized it was Him I was walking towards. He had pursued me everyday, and I had the feeling He would continue to do so for the rest of my life with Him.

Coming to the end of the aisle, I was overwhelmed with excitement. I looked to the One who would wed us, my Father. God, the Father, would be uniting His son and His creation into a perfect union. It was at that moment, I understood the lack of my commitment until this point. Until the wedding, although I had been in a relationship with my Love, I was not fully committed to that relationship.

For so many of us, we are in the relationship but not walking in our designed role. That is why getting married is so important. We cannot become more than the engaged bride unless we commit to the marriage. How are we to know what it looks like to be a wife unless we actually enter into a covenant with our husband?

When I said "I do," it was not my moment of salvation. (Remember I said this could be different for some.) But recall that my moment of salvation was when I agreed to marry Him. I was saying "I do" to the commitment and decision to take upon the role and identity He desired for me. Our identity and role are available the moment of salvation, but we have to make the decision to walk in it to receive its benefits.

If you notice, my Love and I did not repeat the traditional wedding vows most of us are used to hearing: *To have and to hold from this day forward, for better or for worse, for richer, for poorer, in sickness and in health, until death do us part.* While this may be acceptable when marrying your earthly husband, in a marriage to Jesus these vows sound absolutely ridiculous. There is no poorer or richer when you are married to the owner of all wealth. Yes your earthly finances may have gains and losses, but your eternal wealth never decreases. There is no better or worse when your husband is the epitome of perfection. There is no sickness in the marriage to the great physician. Although we experience sickness in this life, He is able to restore our health physically, mentally, and spiritually. And most certainly there is no separation at death between two people who have already died to themselves in order to fully live with each other.

More appropriately spoken in that moment of commitment was the charge of duty from our Heavenly Father to both my Love and me. He called His son to these duties: *"You are to care for her more than you care for yourself. You will sacrifice everything you have, just so she can wake up and have one more day to be my daughter, to be your wife, to be the woman I have desired for her to be. You are to provide for her, to meet her needs. There are times she will run, there are times she will hurt you, there are times she will not want to be with you. Love her anyway. You will love her with a perfect love, yet she will often forget it. You will often protect her when she does not even realize she needs protection. You will pursue her for the rest of her days. You are to die for her so that she may live."*

You know the best part about this moment? My Love's response. He did not answer flippantly or hesitantly, but instead answered sincerely, "With pleasure." And why would I expect anything different from Him? Does not the Word of God say, for the joy set before Him, He endured the cross (Hebrews 12:2)? If it were His joy to endure the cross for me, would He not be more than willing to enter into this covenant? Practically speaking, He had already shown that He was ready when He spread His arms on the cross and died for me. His affirmative response was more for my confirmation than anything else.

And what was my charge: *"You, my daughter, honor him. You will be cared for, provided for, unalterably loved. You will often run from this, but your love will always remain, waiting for your return, ready to forgive. You will be protected, desired, found worthy, and pursued all the days of your life. You need only say, 'I do.'"*

To honor and commit were my only two commands. Everything else had been taken care of already. I needed only to agree and give to my husband the respect and submission due Him. I would be desired? Found worthy? Unalterably loved? What alternative choice would I even consider, but to answer with "I do."

I encourage you to pause and ponder these revelations. Has your relationship with the Lord until this point been based on works and attempts to earn your way to a relationship with Him? By ourselves we are unable to enter into a relationship with Him. It is only through receiving His identity of love and grace that we can walk in an intimate relationship with Him. We are called to say yes; He will take care of the rest. Are you honoring your Husband? If you choose to refuse His gifts, do not deceive yourself, you are dishonoring the Lord and denying Him of His reward for the cross...you. Allow Him to love you, and by honoring Him you will find yourself overflowing with love that cannot be contained. Write your own vows to and from the Lord now. What do you desire to hear Him say and how do you desire to respond?

_____

_____

_____

_____

_____

♥

What's Your Wedding Story?

Now it is your turn. Hopefully you have already been journaling little pieces of your wedding story through this journey. Now put it all together! Spend some time alone with the Lord and allow him to give you the whole picture of your wedding day. Have no expectations. It could look completely different than what He showed me, and that is okay. It is wonderful actually!

What are your vows? What does your dress look like? Who is in the audience? Where do you get married? On the beach, in a church, on a mountain top? How do you feel coming to this moment? Describe in detail everything you see. You never know what He might reveal from the smallest detail. I love each of you so much. Thank you for going this far on the journey with me. Do not stop here. Keep going as we continue our process of becoming beloved.

Section 2: The Ketubah
The Ultimate Love Contract

Identity and Inheritance

In the planning stage of this book, my original intent was to include an in-depth look into Jewish wedding traditions and their correlations to our relationship with Christ. However, the more I sought the Lord's direction for this section, the more I felt the necessity to focus on two specific concepts.

The primary topic to highlight here is our identity as a believer in Christ. Consequently, the second idea explored is the beauty of the Ketubah. In order for us to fully appreciate and understand the Ketubah's significance, we must first understand our identity in Christ. Throughout this section we will explore the role of Jesus as Husband and its implications. We must discover whom we agreed to marry and the inheritance we received when we did, to be secure and confident in our own identity. As believers our basis for identity is rooted in Christ's identity as Husband. Our promises, rights, and privileges derive not from our character or deeds but His. Let's face it, everything returns back to our identity.

♥

Condemnation Be Gone!

There is therefore now no condemnation to those who are in Christ Jesus, who do not walk according to the flesh, but according to the Spirit. Romans 8:1

We need to understand our identity as a believer so we can understand our inheritance. When we understand our inheritance, it will make the Ketubah that much more significant to our journey. "There is therefore now no condemnation for those who are in Christ." Why is this promise significant to us as believers? Understanding we have no condemnation is crucial to our identity as a believer. Freedom from condemnation comes not from learning how to walk blamelessly before God. Freedom from condemnation is a right purchased and provided for by our Husband. It is not a right based on our own merit, but based on Christ's identity and our identity as His chosen wife. We need not earn but only receive by faith.

Our faith. Everything comes back to our belief that the Word of God is truth. Our faith produces our identity and our identity encompasses our inheritance. However, we receive our inheritance through faith (1 Peter 1:3-5). The elements of faith, identity, and inheritance interdependently work together. I believe it is impossible to live our destined life of an overcomer without a revelation of our identity in Christ. However, the revelation of who we are in Christ is only made possible through faith. (We will never be able to justify ourselves; we must humbly receive His blessings.) And without our inheritance (or the promises of God) that we receive through faith, what is the basis of our identity…our own righteousness? Heaven forbid!

> Therefore, brethren, we are debtors—not to the flesh, to live according to the flesh. For if you live according to the flesh you will die; but if by the Spirit you put to death the deeds of the body, you will live. For as many as are led by the Spirit of God, these are sons (daughters) of God. For you did not receive the spirit of bondage again to fear, but you received the Spirit of adoption by whom we cry out, "Abba, Father." The Spirit Himself bears witness with our spirit that we are children of God, and if children, then heirs—heirs of God and joint heirs with Christ, if indeed we suffer with *Him,* that we may also be glorified together. Romans 8:12-17

No longer are we living according to the flesh but according to the Spirit. The Spirit leads us, and because of our adoption by our Father God, we are not in bondage to fear. We are God's children (identity), and we are heirs to His glory (inheritance). Although this may seem obvious, I believe that we often as believers forget to rest in God's grace and enjoy the promised abundant life. Instead, it becomes tempting to desire to work off a debt that is already paid for. With our inheritance, His glory and His name, we become His children and receive our identity. We have been given the right to cry out "Abba Father." He identifies us as His children and what good father does not desire to lavish his children with blessing and love (Matthew 7:7-11)? Imagine a bride refusing to wear her expensive gorgeous engagement ring because of a feeling of unworthiness. She places the ring in its box for protection until she can afford the jewel herself. Needlessly, she toils to repay an imagined debt. All the while rejecting the gift of her beloved and denying them both of much desired intimacy.

Losing condemnation and fear is a significant side effect to gaining our inheritance. Condemnation is to be sentenced, found guilty, and disapproved of.[1] Along with fear, condemnation is what can keep us from walking in our full inheritance. We have not been given bondage to fear but have been made children of God (1 John 4:18). If God is love, then we are children of love. God actually wired us and gifted us for love. When we choose fear instead of love we actually block our inheritance.

Therefore, it is so important that we choose to walk in love, not fear, in our marriage to the Lord so we can receive His full inheritance. It is pertinent to our journey that we grasp the enormity of this concept. We have the ability to be joint heirs with Christ. As a result when we add His existing inheritance to our inheritance that we receive when we chose to walk in faith and love, we receive an abundant reward. What a blessing our God is to give us exceedingly and abundantly all that we could ask or imagine (Ephesians 3:20). Why is this all so important since none of this is new to most of us anyways? Because of the beauty of one simple contract, the Ketubah, in which symbolically we receive our identity and inheritance.

Spend some time in prayer thanking Him for your inheritance. Identify in depth what your inheritance fully entails.

31

_____

_____

♥

The Ketubah

For those of you who are completely uninterested in a history lesson please do not skip this section! We are only going to discuss a little history before diving into the beautiful revelation within the Ketubah. The Ketubah is the Jewish marriage contract that dates back as far as 2500 years ago. It outlines the groom's various responsibilities: to provide his wife with food, shelter, and clothing and be attentive to her emotional needs. The document is signed by two witnesses and has the standing of a legally binding agreement. The Ketubah is the property of the bride, and she must have access to it throughout their marriage.[2]

Sample Ketubah contract:

"On the _____ day of the week, the _____ day of the month _____ in the year _____ since the creation of the world according to the reckoning which we are accustomed to use here in the city of _____ in _____. _____ son of _____ of the family _____ said to this maiden _____ daughter of _____ of the family _____ 'Be thou my wife according to the law of Moses and Israel. I will work for thee, honor, provide for, and support thee, in accordance with the practice of Jewish husbands, who work for their wives, honor, provide for and support them in truth. I will set aside for thee (a certain amount of money) due thee for thy maidenhood, which belongs to thee, and thy food, clothing, and other necessary benefits which a husband is obligated to provide; and I will live with thee in accordance with the requirements prescribed for each husband."[3] (*modified*)

Throughout the wedding ceremony, there are several symbolic gestures that occur. The reading of the Ketubah acts as a break between the first part of the ceremony, the betrothal and the latter part, the marriage. The Ketubah is given to the bride as a promise of protection and provision. One of the ways for a Jewish marriage to be validated is through the passing of the contract, a bride's acceptance of the Ketubah. That is the reason for requiring witnesses to observe the handoff of the Ketubah.[4]

Her role is to receive the document, but she neither has to sign the document or promise anything except to become the wife. This contract serves as the groom's sign of self-sacrifice so that his bride is cared for during their marriage. The bride merely receives the document. Often in the Jewish wedding ceremony the exchanging of the rings either precedes or is done simultaneously along with the reading of the Ketubah. What I love about the wedding band in our culture today is how it serves as a seal for the engagement ring. When the wedding band is placed on the finger it represents the decision to enter into a covenant together. The bride receives the seal of the covenant (identity) and listens to the promise of her inheritance.

Through this simple contract and exchanging of something valuable, the rings, we see a real life example of the truth in Romans. The bride receives her identity through the covenant seal given through the rings and her inheritance through the reading of the Ketubah. Why am I making such an emphasis on the Ketubah? Let us take this one step further.

Jesus is the Ketubah. This blows me away! Think about it. He is the contract that allows us to become the bride of Christ. When Jesus died on the cross for us, He became our physical, emotional, and spiritual fulfillment. The only thing we have to do is receive him. Just as the bride's only obligation is to choose to receive the contract and enter into a covenant of marriage with her groom, our only duty is to enter into a relationship with the Father.

For generations, there was a separation (the veil in the tabernacle) between God and His children (Exodus 26:33). However, Jesus came and died on the cross and that veil was torn, and the barrier between God and man was destroyed forever (Matthew 27:51). Jesus came and made Himself to be the contract so that we can enter into an intimate relationship with Him with no separation. Just as we exchange something valuable in rings, God exchanged what He valued most, His son Jesus, for us. As we enter into a covenant relationship with Jesus, the Father places the seal of the Holy Spirit (ring) upon our fingers as our representation of the covenant and our identity (Ephesians 1:13, 4:30). Therefore, the two witnesses who sign and validate the contract are the Father and the Holy Spirit.

Also, take note of the provision that Jesus is providing for us here as His bride. When we enter into a marriage with Him, we are receiving what is His inheritance as well as the peace of knowing that we are always going to be cared for by our Husband. This is why it is so important to know our inheritance as a believer. We truly understand what we gain with the receipt of the Ketubah. Every need we could have will be provided for; all we have to do is reach out our hand and receive the contract.

*I challenge you to investigate other Jewish wedding customs in your time with the Lord today and see what other fresh revelations come to you. *Hint you could start with looking up the Badeken, Chuppah, Seudah, etc. Also see the Notes section at the end of the book for sources I used during my study. But I am serious, take and journal what you gained from the Ketubah and your own personal study time.*

_____

_____

_____

_____

_____

♥

Do You Know Who My Husband Is?

Hopefully these last sections really grabbed a hold of your heart and encouraged your confidence. When we can really grasp who are Husband is, there is absolutely no reason for a lack of assurance. Knowing who and whose we are as believers is so important to understanding our identity as the bride of Christ. For this reason, I am able to be open and honest with you about my walk with the Lord. I know my identity and His love for me so there is no shame in what anyone thinks of me. When we are married to Jesus and are walking in and believing His promise for our inheritance, there is nothing else in which we need. But do we have the faith to believe and walk in that identity?

For example, imagine an extremely wealthy and well-known man. We will call him Donald for the purpose of this illustration. Donald's wife goes to a car dealership and picks out the most expensive car on the lot. When the salesman approaches the wife, he does not know who she is or that her husband is Donald. The salesman says to her, "Excuse me, but do you know how much that car is?" She then responds to him, "Do you know who my husband is?"

Now I know this is a funny example, but I do not think we understand just how often this happens in our spiritual lives. Have you ever been in a certain season of your life where things were difficult or seemingly impossible? During that time did a test of faith arrive in the form of a well-intentioned family member or friend asking, "Do you not see what is going on here? What you are believing for is ridiculous." For most of us, the answer is yes. In fact, it probably happens more often than we actually realize.

When that does happen, what is your response? Do you believe them and their declaration of the impossibility of your situation? Do you give into your fear? Or with every bit of confidence do you ask yourself, "Do I know who my Husband is? Do I not think He has the best intentions for me?" Understand I am not discrediting the need for reason or submitting our dreams to the Lord. Without logic, how could we identify the miraculous? The difference is that faith trumps logic. Now trust me when I say I realize this is a lot easier said theoretically than actually practiced in the moment of difficulty. How are we able to stand with certainty in that instance? Because we know our identity as the bride of Christ and we have faith in our Husband's character and judgment. Why else would it be important that we received our inheritance when we accepted Jesus? There is so much more to our inheritance than what we receive when we are in Heaven one day, for instance the abundant life.

If we only half-heartedly believe our marriage to Jesus allows us to become joint heirs with Him, then we will not have the confidence and security to face those trials and stand on the foundation of our Husband's identity. However, because we choose to believe in the marriage contract that was given to us and through faith believe for our inheritance, nothing within us needs to be in bondage to fear. Instead, we have all of the confidence in the world to believe for love, trust, and truth. We are confident our Husband is true to His Word.

However, let us suppose this wife married her husband out of obligation, and she never spent time getting to know him or his character. So one day, her husband asks her to go buy a new car for them. Only when she gets to the dealership she has no idea of her budget, what kind of car would please her husband, or what purpose the car will serve. She is at a loss because she never got to know her husband.

It is so often the same in our relationship with our Love. Jesus is true to His Word. He will provide for all of our needs-- physically, emotionally, and spiritually, but how much easier would it be to be confident in Him, if we took the time to really get to know His character. So again, I ask you, "Do you know who your Husband is?"

Spend some quality time with your Husband today. How does His Word demonstrate His identity? His role? His provision? His character? Is the Holy Spirit revealing any aspects of Jesus or your relationship with Him that you have not fully grasped or rested in?

_____

_____

_____

_____

_____

♥

Role Play

Wives, understand and support your husbands in ways that show your support for Christ. The husband provides leadership to his wife the way Christ does to His church, not by domineering but by cherishing. So just as the church submits to Christ as He exercises such leadership, wives should likewise submit to their husbands.

Husbands, go all out in your love for your wives, exactly as Christ did for the church—a love marked by giving, not getting. Christ's love makes the church whole. His words evoke her beauty. Everything He does and says is designed to bring the best out of her, dressing her in dazzling white silk, radiant with holiness. And that is how husbands ought to love their wives. They are really doing themselves a favor— since they are already "one" in marriage.

No one abuses his own body, does he? No, he feeds and pampers it. That's how Christ treats us, the church, since we are part of his body. And this is why a man leaves father and mother and cherishes his wife. No longer two, they become "one flesh." This is a huge mystery, and I don't pretend to understand it all. What is clearest to me is the way Christ treats the church. And this provides a good picture of how each husband is to treat his wife, loving himself in loving her, and how each wife is to honor her husband. Ephesians 5:22-33 The Message

How are we to understand an earthly marriage if we ignore the spiritual marriage Christ created for us? This question will become relevant to us throughout the rest of the book as we discover more and more the reality of having Christ as our Husband. However, not only are we concerned with knowing Christ as our personal Husband, but someday (if not already married) we will be entering into an earthly marriage. I truly believe He gave us this passage in Ephesians to remind us of His original plan for marriage. Just as we discussed earlier in Section One, we see the need for honor and love mirrored within this beautiful passage of scripture, as they play key parts in the husband's and wife's role.

Beginning with the role of the wife: understand and support your husband as you would Christ. I love the use of the word "understand." How do we understand Christ? We get to know him. We discover what pleases Him, upsets Him, and excites Him. We take the time to develop knowledge of His Word and His heart for us. In the same way, we as women should strive to understand our husbands. We are able to have a greater respect for something that we truly understand.

In addition to understanding, we are called to support. Support is a key word for this topic of respecting and understanding the husband. Support means "to bear or hold up, to sustain or withstand without giving way; serve as a prop for, and to undergo or endure, especially with patience or submission."[5] How exhilarating it is for us to understand our privilege as the wife to support and serve as a helper for our husband. The definition of support leads to the next role for the wife which is to submit. It is our extreme honor as a woman to be able to submit to our husbands, just as it is to submit to God. When we submit to our husband, we allow ourselves to walk in a blessing from the Lord and our husband to walk in his designed role as leader. Every part of our role as the wife, produces honor for the husband.

Now the husband's role is founded on loving the wife. He is to love her through his actions and his words just as Christ loves the church. His words for the wife are to awaken, strengthen, and shine light on her inner and outer beauty. Just as Christ's love for the church is not with the purpose to receive anything in return, the husband's role is not to love with expectations. Instead, he is to love her with a self-sacrificing love. Just as the wife's role is to honor the husband, the husband's is built on loving the wife.

Here again, we find the two principles of love and honor. The two things asked for in the vows from *The Wedding* in Section One, remember? Love and honor! The beauty in Ephesians is that when you do these things for your spouse, because you are "one," in essence you receive the blessing of your obedience. This is how the Lord works; when you are obedient to His way of doing something, you reap the blessing of your effort. Therefore, wives honor your husband and you will be loved. Husbands love your wives so you will be honored. When you do these things with pure intentions, you will find that you receive both honor and love—exactly what Christ displays for us through our relationship with Him.

One more desire of my heart for us, as women, to understand is the stunning image of being a wife found in Proverbs. This is how I long to be described one day when I am a wife and mother: a classy woman who brings honor to her family in all areas of their lives.

A good woman is hard to find,
 and worth far more than diamonds.
Her husband trusts her without reserve,
 and never has reason to regret it.
Never spiteful, she treats him generously
 all her life long…
She's up before dawn, preparing breakfast
 for her family and organizing her day…
 rolls up her sleeves, eager to get started.
She senses the worth of her work,
 is in no hurry to call it quits for the day.
She's skilled in the crafts of home and hearth,
 diligent in homemaking.
She's quick to assist anyone in need,
 reaches out to help the poor…
Her husband is greatly respected
 when he deliberates with the city fathers…
Her clothes are well-made and elegant,
 and she always faces tomorrow with a smile.
When she speaks she has something worthwhile to say,
 and she always says it kindly.
She keeps an eye on everyone in her household,
 and keeps them all busy and productive.
Her children respect and bless her;
 her husband joins in with words of praise:
"Many women have done wonderful things,
 but you've outclassed them all!"
Charm can mislead and beauty soon fades.
 The woman to be admired and praised
 is the woman who lives in the Fear-of-GOD.
Give her everything she deserves!
 Festoon her life with praises!
Proverbs 31:10-31 The Message (selected verses)

It is my heart for us as women to understand the reward that comes with striving for this ideal. What wife and mother (or future wife and mother) would not desire to hear her children and husband sing praises of her effort? Again, however, we note that she honors her husband and household by understanding their needs and meeting them. She supports her husband by caring for him and working in a way that allows him to be respected amongst others. When done with pure intentions, i.e. sensing the worth of her work and always facing tomorrow with a smile, we find the honor returned back to her. One translation states it this way, "Her children rise up and call her blessed; her husband also, and he praises her, 'Many have done well, but you excel them all.'(Proverbs 31:28-29, NKJV)."

Not only can I strive for the respect and love of my earthly husband, but my Husband, Jesus, already praises and encourages me. One day I will actually get to hear him say "Well done my good and faithful servant (Matthew 25:21)." So my beautiful sisters, honor so that you may be honored and love so that you may be loved. This is your role as wife. What a joy and privilege!

♥

Section 3: The Love Stories
Being the Wife

Move In Together

The purpose of this next section is to allow you an opportunity to experience the romance of Jesus as Husband. Now that the wedding has taken place, there is a marriage to be lived. Saying "I do" is not the end of the story. In fact, it is merely the beginning.

♥

Imagine two young people completely in love with each other. The young man picks up his girlfriend every Friday and Saturday night for a romantic evening full of wonderful surprises. The more time they spend with one another, the more they desire to constantly be together. However, at the end of each date, as is proper, the young man must bring his beloved home to her house and return to his. The next weekend the beloved anxiously waits for her love to come pick her up for another blessed adventure. Again, the end of the evening comes where he must drop his beloved back to her home. This dating season continues for quite some time, until they finally receive her parents' blessing to marry.

The wedding is planned, and finally the day comes for the two to be united in marriage. Vows are spoken, rings are exchanged, and a glorious reception is held to celebrate the joining of two such lovely people. After the reception is over and all the guests go home, the husband and wife get into his vehicle. They are overwhelmed with love for one another and excited for this new journey ahead. As the night draws to a close, the groom drives his new wife to her house, kisses her good night, gets back in his car, and drives home. The wife thinks nothing of it but goes inside and gets ready for bed, awaiting the next time her husband will come.

Such a sweet story right? Wrong! This is absolutely absurd. When two people get married, there is a oneness that happens. The two will live in the *same* house. He no longer has to drop her off at the end of the date. He gets to park the car and come inside to the place they dwell together.

However, how often does this occur in our spiritual lives? We have great days with the Lord, whether it is through a worship service, a moment of excitement, an answered prayer, or just a sweet encounter between God and us. Yet at the end of the day, we come back to our homes, go to sleep, and wait for another spiritual experience. We are living our daily lives the best we know how. Everything we do throughout our day, we do to honor and glorify the One we love, but at the end of the day, we are still coming home and not choosing to live with our Husband.

It is not because we do not *want* to live with Him. On the contrary, just as the young couple went back to their separate homes after they were married, we habitually leave our wedded bliss to return to our pre-covenant state. You know the saying "We are creatures of habit?" It's true! Unless we consciously break that habit, we will constantly keep doing it. For so long we lived as the dating couple or even the engaged couple, but now that we are married and fully committed, does our life look any different?

Jesus is not like the man in the story; he does not desire to take us to our own home at the end of the evening. Instead, Jesus is true to His character and will wait for you to make the decision to box up your things and make the move.

♥

So pack your bags because you are moving out! Here is what I find special about what we learned in the previous section, The Ketubah: The only things you need to take to your new place are the gifts He gave you since the moment you were engaged. The little stuffed animals He won on your dates, the bracelet He bought for your anniversary, the pictures of the two of you, pack them up. Everything else you will need, He has already provided for you. Think back to the contract He signed which states that He will provide shelter, food, and clothing, all of your needs.

Remember how my agreement to marry Him represents my salvation? From that point He has been showering me with gifts to enable me to better understand our relationship and my role as His helpmate. While in an earthly relationship those might be stuffed animals and jewelry, but in a relationship with Jesus those gifts could be teaching, ministry, encouragement, and so on.

Once you move in with Him, He will continue to provide for you and even begin to give more gifts such as faith, healing, discernment, etc. (1 Corinthians 12:1-11). When He sees you are faithful with the gifts He has already given you, He begins to entrust you with even more (Matthew 25:23). It is time to break the habit of going back to your own house. Take the next step and dwell with Him. Come into an even closer fellowship with Him. Look forward to coming home with Him at the end of the day. He will anxiously await for you to sit down and speak with Him for hours. He is such a faithful Husband.

So what might this look like practically for you? That is the part you get to decide. Make your relationship with the Christ every bit as personal as you desire with an earthly husband. This will—and should—vary greatly between people. For you single ladies it could be that you literally come home, walk through the door, and greet Him with, "Honey I'm home." Obviously, this would be impractical for a woman married with children. Your family would think you had lost your mind!

I think it is so much more the attitude of the heart that God is after in this stage. Ask yourself: Are my heart and mind remaining connected with Jesus, or am I separating at any time to independently make decisions like a single woman? Your Husband longs to be near you every moment of everyday. He literally is the Husband we all secretly wish for, who waits for us to get home just to hear us speak to Him. Just so He can hear our voice. Please take time to think what form this might take for you. Open your heart; Jesus is waiting.

♥

The Love Stories

(A 14 Day Devotional: Moments with Your Husband)

My heart's desire is that after reading these next few stories you will gain a greater understanding of the romantic and creative sides of Jesus. Since the day I was given the vision of the wedding and realized my answer was yes to join with Him as His wife, He has taken me on so many adventures. Again, some of these stories are simply visions that He gave me, some are stories of my convictions after becoming His wife, and others are actual dates I allowed the Lord to take me on. In a few instances, you will see the reality of my relationship with the Lord. It is not meant to be overly dramatic for the sake of a good story or cause you to compare your relationship with the Lord to mine. He works in each of us differently.

With each story, see the depth of relationship that is available. So often I am asked the question, "What does it look like practically to walk as the bride of Christ?" (Remember, the Lord still sees me as His bride even though I am now the married bride.) This is why the process of becoming the bride of Christ is a continuous journey. It would be easy to get caught up in finding so-called *practical* ways to walk as the bride, but then it would not be the unique and romantic relationship we all desire. Our marriage to the Lord will be more than we could have ever dreamed possible. The only probable thing about our relationship is that He will never leave us, never stop loving us, and never go back on His promises (Hebrews 13:5,8). The way He pursues us each day is something new and wonderful to be discovered continuously. Therefore, our marriage (not the wedding) to Him is a daily process. Marriage is deciding everyday to wake up next to Him, spend our day honoring Him, come home everyday, and fall asleep next to Him. It is the little things *He* will do that make the decision so worth it.

I have a suggestion. Take the next few stories and read one a day. Allow this section of the book to really serve as a devotional time for the next two weeks. At the end of each story, ask the Holy Spirit what He desires to speak to you specifically during that story. Remember most of these are just thoughts and visions I have had throughout my life. You are getting a chance to see my walk with the Lord up close and personal. But as you should with anything, please test all things and hold on only to what is good (1 John 4:1). The things that speak to you and minister to your spirit, ponder on them (Philippians 4:8). Allow the revelation the Lord gives you to soak in, and on the sections that do not speak to you, move on. Ask the Lord for your own story for that day. He will give it to you. Pray this prayer at the beginning of each day:

Beloved Jesus, speak to my heart these next few moments. Romance me in a special way today. Remind me today of your desire to walk with me as Husband. I love you. ~Your beloved

♥

Would You Like to Go Out with Me Sometime?

Day 1

I remember the day after God gave me the vision of the wedding day from Section One. Everything felt sweet and new. I felt overjoyed at the idea about being married. It was so lovely. The possibilities with Him seemed endless. During the day as I was spending time with my Love, I heard Him ask me. "Would you like to go out with Me sometime?" Sounds silly I know, but this actually happened.

"Sure," I answered. Just a few days before, I had thought about starting a new devotional and finished writing on the last page of my journal. Therefore, I was in need of some new material. I decided to go to a local Christian bookstore in the area to shop for my new items and spend some time with Jesus.

The next morning I woke up before anyone else in my apartment. I put on a simple but cute dress and drove to the bookstore. For the next two hours, I sat on the floor of the bookstore reading and silently speaking to the Lord about which devotional He would have me choose. He finally directed me to a different section of the store where the Bible reading plans were kept. I had read through the Bible many times before, Genesis to Revelation, so I was a little confused as to why He led me there. Skimming across the different journals, I came across a chronological plan of the Bible. It was a guide to reading through the Bible in the order scholars believed it had been written. Not only that, but it was a journal in which to write my thoughts about each section of scripture I would read. I felt very strongly this was the one He wanted me to purchase. Proud of my selection, I went up to the register, purchased the book, and drove to the nearest coffee shop.

Once at the coffee shop, I asked the Lord again, "Why this choice?" He plainly said to me, "You have read through the Bible before and seen Me as Savior, Healer, Provider, and Almighty. This time I want you to read it as My beloved and watch Me unveil Myself to you as Redeemer, as your Love, and as your Husband." Speechless, I finished my coffee and headed back home marveling at the beautiful first date I experienced as a wife.

For me, a bookstore and a coffee shop was a wonderful first date.

However, for you a wonderful date might be mountain biking, attending a concert in the park, or going to a museum. Whatever it is, listen to Him. I imagine He wants to ask you, "Would you like to go out with me sometime?" My challenge to you today, go on some sort of date with your Husband and get to know Him like you would if you were on an actual first date. Plan it now. Sometime within the next week, go on a date with Him. Then come back and journal about your experience.

_____

_____

_____

_____

_____

♥

Rubies and Pearls

Day 2

Who can find a virtuous wife? For her worth is far above rubies.
The heart of her husband safely trusts here. Proverbs 31:10-11

A few weeks before I turned eighteen my parents asked me what I wanted for my birthday. The year I turned eighteen there was this new trend developing, the purity ring. There was one ring in particular many people started wearing, which represented their vow to stay sexually pure until marriage. Several of my friends had started wearing these rings, and although I too had made a vow to save sex for marriage, I was not sure I wanted to wear the ring. The theme of the ring did not seem to say exactly what I wanted it to mean. While I absolutely love the idea of this particular ring, I knew I wanted something a little different than the norm. So when my parents asked me what I wanted, I was able to tell them I wanted a ruby ring. I had a read a verse in Proverbs about a virtuous wife being worth more than rubies. Therefore, I decided I wanted a ruby ring for my birthday.

My mother and I drove to a small jewelry store and began to look at their selection. I finally picked one out that was a very simple heart shaped ruby on a gold band. I still wear it to this day, and I will wear it until the day I marry my earthly prince. Something I would later realize about the significance of the ring choice was that I wanted far more than to wait to have sex until marriage. I wanted to proclaim my vow to stay emotionally pure for my husband as well. I knew even by that age, adultery began in the heart. Proverbs 23:7 says "That which a man does in his heart, so is he."

I wanted to be able to give to my husband more than just a pure body. By no means am I against dating. Please do not arrive at that conclusion. However, what I am saying is that I want to be cautious with whom I give my heart to. As women, we are so quick to give ourselves away emotionally. This often damages us so much that we require spiritual healing as if we had physically given into the temptation. Matthew 7:6 challenges us: "Do not give what is holy to the dogs, nor cast your pearls before the pigs." Your pearl is much more than physical virtue. Virtue is defined as "characterized by or possessing virtue or moral excellence, righteous, upright; chaste."[6] It goes much deeper than the physical; moral excellence is a part of your character.

While I wish I could say I have never emotionally given myself away since placing that ring on my finger, that is simply not the case. I chose that ring years before I would have the revelation of the wedding day. But if you recall, I told you about the men chasing me in the field. Each one of them was a representation of the men I had at some point invested my heart into. However, I often wonder if I had not set the standard where I did, how many more men would have been chasing me that day? How much harder would it have been to outrun them to the steps of the church?

My beloved sister, He is not trying to set impossible standards for you. Do not believe the lie that because you cannot change the past there is no point striving for purity now. This is not the case. Do you recall, He shut the door of the church, leaving the men outside? He restored your gown. It is white, and you are royalty. Walk in it!

Do not feel guilty for having feelings for a man. That is where legalism comes in. He gave us those feelings. They are a blessing. Though I caution you to watch how far you invest in those feelings before God has given permission. "Do not stir up or awaken love until it pleases" Song of Solomon 2:7.

What is the Holy Spirit saying to you? Has there been a time when you have given yourself either physically or emotionally to a man? If so it is not too late to ask God to heal your heart so you can start anew.

♥

Man of Honor, Woman of Excellence

Day 3

Now, my daughter, do not fear. I will do for you whatever you ask, for all my people in the city know that you are a woman of excellence. Ruth 3:11 (NASB)

If you have not read the book of Ruth now is my encouragement to put this book down and pick up your Bible. Read through the book of Ruth today and pick this book back up tomorrow. I am convinced there is enough in that story to keep you thrilled for days. If you are familiar with the story, then feel free to continue with today's devotion.

Let's jump right into the story, starting with Boaz. I like to picture Boaz as a strong, mature, and rather handsome individual. One night, he is sleeping peacefully, only to be awakened to find a woman sleeping at the end of his bed. Ruth, a widowed woman with nothing left, in obedience to her mother-in-law's instructions, has uncovered the feet of a stranger and lain next to him. In the story, we discover that Ruth is in need of redemption and through her actions, has demonstrated her submission to Boaz as her choice for the source of her redemption.

What we are able to see about our relationship with the Lord through this story is the beauty of honor. Ruth bestows honor to Boaz by following instructions and lying humbly at his feet. In response to her honor and submission, he promises to protect her honor as well. He states that "the city will know her as a woman of excellence." I believe that Ruth's honor which was rooted in obedience, allowed Boaz to become her redeemer. The last section of this story in my Bible is titled, *Boaz redeems Ruth*. I love that! Is that not exactly what my Love did for me? When I submitted fully to Him, His full redemption was mine.

Psalm 45:11 reads, "So the King will greatly desire your beauty; because He is your Lord worship Him." He finds us beautiful. Not only that, but this clearly states that he desires us. *He desires you.* As women, we long not only to be needed but also wanted. The King of all the earth finds your beauty captivating. So much so, He lived His life so He could redeem you. At the cost of His life, He chose you and me.

Did you notice what the verse in Psalms described as His desired response from us? Worship, which can also be defined as rendering honor and respect. Do you remember the one thing the Father charged me with on our wedding day? He told me I was to honor my Love.

Boaz could have said no to Ruth's request for redemption, but he saw her to be a woman of excellence and desired to redeem her. The cycle of honor here is so beautiful. God's honor for us came through the sacrifice of His son Jesus. Our honor in return is through obedience and commitment to Him.

What aspects of Ruth's story spoke to you? How do you show honor to your Husband? What are some new ways you could honor Him? With your words, attitudes, actions, faith, obedience, trust? Elaborate on these thoughts and do not forget, write them down! You are doing well. I love you dear friend!

♥

A Day at the Spa
Day 4

Do not let your adornment be merely outward-the arranging of hair, wearing gold, or putting on fine apparel—rather let it be the hidden person of the heart, with the incorruptible beauty of a gentle and quiet spirit, which is very precious in the sight of God. 1 Peter 3:3-4

One of my favorite things to do is to go get my hair done in the morning. There is nothing like waking up and knowing you are heading to the salon. The way they massage your hair with the shampoo, which always smells way better than your own, relaxes me to the core. In my opinion, here are the ingredients for a great Saturday morning: Leisurely wake up, drink coffee, go to the salon, come back home, pick out a cute outfit, apply makeup, and enjoy!

Seriously, does that not sound wonderful? But what about the verse in 1 Peter that tells us not to do those things. Take a closer look: "Do not let your adornment be *merely* outward....rather let it be...." I love looking at the definition of words. It really helps to bring truth to common areas of misconception. Take the word *merely* for example: "only as specified and nothing more; simply."[7]

Let's read the verse again replacing the word merely. "Do not let your adornment be only and nothing more than outward..." That completely changes the verse's meaning. I love it! It allows me to enjoy makeup, cute clothes, jewelry, etc. guilt free. And trust me I do! But wait. If I am going to take the first part of this verse into consideration, I should take the second part as well.

"Let (your adornment) be the hidden person of the heart, with the incorruptible beauty of a gentle and quiet spirit, which is very precious in the sight of God." I wonder how many of you for years have heard that verse and felt so constricted and frustrated by it. Could it be that since the moment we read the verse a lie was already settling its way into us?

I truly believe this verse is supposed to be liberating for us as women, not suffocating. I remember the times I would get so excited about something or passionate over a certain issue when talking with my friends, but I would come home at the end of the day feeling embarrassed. I was not behaving in the manner of a gentle and quiet person when speaking out my passions. (By the way notice it says spirit, not person. Just making sure you are paying attention!)

This is exactly the way the enemy would have wanted me to feel. The enemy wanted me to believe that because I am a girl, I should just sit around, have no opinion, smile and nod my head when appropriate in order to obey the Word of God. However, it was not until I began to study about the character of a woman and wife, that I read this verse in a completely new light.

Instead of feeling limited and bound, I now read this verse as permission to be sought after while being completely myself. Seriously, "let it be the hidden person of the heart." If something is hidden, it must be searched for in order to be found. I was to adorn myself with the character of a submitted woman, which we learned earlier is liberating not condemning. I do not have to do anything to demonstrate my value. Not even to the Lord. If it were up to me to become worthy, I would be lost forever. However, because of His blood that washes over me, I am able to be found by Him and enter into a covenant relationship with Him.

And about this whole "gentle and quiet spirit." Let's think about it this way. When you are in a romantic relationship with someone and you long to tell them how much you love them, do you scream your confession of love at them? Are you rough in your deliverance? When you are genuinely in love are you angry all the time? Prone to outbursts? The answer to all of these is no, of course not! Quiet when used as a verb, simply means to make tranquil or peaceful or to calm mentally.[8] Gentleness means not severe, rough or violent. Synonyms for gentle are peaceful, tender, and merciful.[9]

When I speak to my Love and tell Him how much I love Him, I do not yell at Him and neither does He to me. In fact, my love for Him often comes in a tenderness and peacefulness in my spirit. My Love does not come up behind me and scream "I LOVE YOU" in my ear, frightening me in the process. No, instead He gently and affectionately, in order to mentally calm me, tells me He loves me. He tells me He greatly desires my beauty and His banner over me is love (Song of Solomon 2:4). Oh the incorruptible beauty of a gentle and quiet spirit. How precious it is in the sight of God.

In what ways has your Husband romanced you today? How has He spoken of His love for you? In return, how will you tell Him or your love for Him? Like an earthly marriage, roadblocks can be set up that hinder romance. Have you been reading any verses with a misleading interpretation? Remember His Word is only to bring you freedom and sometimes conviction, but never guilt and condemnation. Identify possible blocks (lies) about your character, and hear His voice speaking to you today.

_____

_____

_____

♥

My Patient Husband

Day 5

How is he so patient? He is the most amazing, beautiful, creative, and romantic man I know. Everyday I wake up knowing His deep desire to pursue me, to call me His own, and every evening I fall asleep thinking "Why me?" Do you ever think that? Really, married or single, do you ever wonder if there really is a perfect person out there ready to love you with everything in them. I know we discussed the idea of a perfect Husband earlier, but have you really thought about it? His perfection is never meant to make you feel inferior, but instead bold and confident in your Love's strength.

Every morning as I wake up and every night as I fall asleep, I know that He is there whispering His loving thoughts into my ears.... the only problem is, sometimes I am not listening. You see, I have this problem of thinking too much. Partly because I am a girl (okay, mostly because I am a girl) and partly because I am thinker, dreamer, and wisher. But that is exactly who He desires for me to be when my thoughts, dreams, and hopes are on Him. The problem is often my selfish and prideful desires get in the way of having those perfect thoughts of Him. These sins (selfishness and pride) hinder me from the most amazing relationship a person could ever ask for. However, He never fails. With one word He reminds me to clear my head, to focus on His eyes—His beautiful eyes—and listen. And with one word from his mouth I am swept away again. My mind is refocused, my heart is made new, and my harmony is restored. If only this routine of being refocused did not have to happen so often. No matter how many times I remind myself of His love, my silly stubbornness again distracts me from His gaze. So my sweet Jesus thank you for being so patient. For always standing there with your arms wide open to receive me no matter how many times I turn away from you. Help me to remember to wake up every morning with the desire of *becoming beloved.*

What are some sins in your life that cause you to cyclically doubt or loose focus? How can you refocus on His beautiful eyes and make your heart new again? He is longing to speak to you and give you peace. Are you focused enough to hear?

♥

The Way He Holds My Hand
Day 6

This is what my Beloved spoke to me...

"Take hold my love. Feel the way your heart flutters when I grab your hand...guess what, my heart does the same. If only you could see the smile that comes across your face when I whisper into your ear, 'Come away my love.' Oh that smile, it is the joy of my heart. My beloved, I love to lead you. I love to grab your hand and lead you into fascinating places. I love to be your protector. When your enemies come against you, my defenses go up. Nothing will harm you my love, because I have set my best guards on all sides of us. Our relationship is stronger than any force the world could throw our direction. Our love conquers. When you worry, my love, my heart aches. I wish you knew how much

I desire to lavish you with blessings. All the desires of your heart, those are mine too. You are my beloved, and I am yours.

Come with me, my love. Let me tell you a story.

'There was once a prince who was married to the most dazzling princess. The prince led her by the hand on their journey to the kingdom, to dwell in the most magnificent and extravagant castle in all the land. However, in order to get to this castle, they had to pass through the enchanted forest. In this forest were many dark, unfamiliar, and foreign places. From time to time, the princess would get so focused on those dark places that she would forget whose hand she held. Fear and doubt would flood the princess to the point she felt she was being overcome. Then she would feel the warmth of her beloved's hand in hers, and with the squeeze of his hand she would turn her head, gaze into his eyes, and forget all of her fears. How could she be fearful, she was holding the hand of the prince? It was then when she took her eyes off the dark places, she remembered the purpose of the journey. Peace restored, she was able to see the delightful places the prince was trying to lead her. Who would have known there were stunning waterfalls, flourishing gardens, rivers with lush greenery flowing along the most magnificent mountains, here along this journey? It was as if the dark places of the enchanted forest turned into vast spaces of glorious freedom when she gazed into her prince's eyes. You see it was here that the prince was able to show the princess how wonderful the journey to the kingdom was when she kept her gaze upon him....'

You see my love, this story, well... it is you and me. I am the Prince and you are my beautiful princess. My love, I am leading you to the most wonderful castle you could ever imagine. So please come away with me. Let me lead you to the happily ever after... It will come. I promise, it is coming. But until then, come with me, hold my hand, and *become my beloved*."

What dark unfamiliar places is your Prince taking you through in order to get to your grand castle? Do you trust Him to lead you there and feel Him holding your hand? Have you focused only on the dark place and forgotten to see the breathtaking scenery within your view?

_____

_____

_____

_____

_____

♥

Sweet Nothings in My Ear

Day 7

My beloved spoke and said to me: "Rise up, my love, my fair one, and come away!" Song of Solomon 2:10

Remember from Day 4 how we discussed the romantic way the Lord speaks to us? Well, today is all about hearing what He speaks when He whispers in our ear. Before we allow the Truth to engulf us, let me mention one thing.

Growing up I had a difficult time with boys; I never dated and still to this day have never been in a serious romantic relationship. Prior to college, there were only a handful of times that I could remember a guy showing interest in me, and never once did I hear I was beautiful from any male except from a few men in my family (Thanks Dad!).

When I began college, I found the most amazing group of friends a girl could have. The girls were encouraging and consistent in their friendship, and the guys actually took the time to compliment the girls in our circle of friends.

The guys' compliments were completely innocent and rooted in a motive to build us up as sisters in Christ. They would say simple things like: "Jennifer, you look very pretty today." "Is that a new outfit? It looks very nice on you." "You are a wonderful, beautiful woman of the Lord." Do you understand no man (besides family) had ever told me I was pretty? So when my friends told me these things I did not know how to handle it. A lot of times I would avoid the comment all together or brush it off like it never happened. Why? Honestly, I did not really believe them. It was not until one day one of them stopped me and said, "Do you realize that you *are* beautiful? This is truth and not something we say just to be kind."

That day changed my life forever. It was not my friend who stopped me that day; it was the Lord who sweetly spoke to me through him. My entire concept of myself as a beautiful woman, fearfully and wonderfully made, was transformed (Psalms 139:14). I began to receive the love of the Lord in a new way.

Some of you have never heard you are beautiful. Hear it from the Lord today. He is longing to romance and tell you how lovely you are to Him. How will you hear His romance spoken over you today? As He comes behind you to whisper in your ear, will you choose to believe what He desires to speak? What good does it do for us to hear a truth and not believe it? How can we be truly changed by His romance if we do not believe the love being spoken over us is truth? As you read each scripture, really ponder over it and hear your Beloved's voice. I love you my gorgeous sister.

Your Beloved Speaks:

- ♥ Let me see your face, let me hear your voice, for your voice is sweet, and your face is lovely. Song of Solomon 2:14
- ♥ How precious are my thoughts to you my love. How great is the sum of them! Psalms 139:17
- ♥ Dear, dear friend and lover, you're as beautiful as Tirzah, city of delights, lovely as Jerusalem, city of dreams, the ravishing visions of my ecstasy. Your beauty is too much for me—I'm in over my head. Song of Solomon 6:4-5 The Message
- ♥ I the King am greatly enthralled by your beauty. Psalms 45:11 *paraphrased*
- ♥ You are more than a conqueror through Me who loves you…. *Nothing* will be able to separate you from my love. Romans 8:37-39 *paraphrased*
- ♥ My love is patient and kind. I am not proud or rude. Neither

am I selfish. I am not easily angered. I think no evil of you. I do not rejoice in your iniquity, but I rejoice in My truth. I always protect. I always trust. I always hope, and I always persevere. I never fail. 1 Corinthians 13:4-8 *paraphrased*

_____

_____

_____

_____

_____

♥

Daydreamer, My Rescuer

Day 8

This is for the daydreamers like myself. Have you ever at some point had a daydream of being in distress, and the man of your dreams comes in and saves the day? Yes? I know I sure have! I believe that God sometimes uses our imagination to speak to us. Personally, I love to be out in nature, alone with Jesus. One day I was hiking through some hills, spending the morning in the wilderness with my Love. I slowly breathed in the crisp cool air of autumn that seemed to dance across the hills rustling the newly turned golden leaves. Even more peaceful was a still calm voice speaking to my heart. It was a precious time with my Love. A few days later, during my drive home for Thanksgiving, my recent adventure in the hills sparked a most interesting **daydream**:

I was back in the hills, only this time I was on a mission. I was not really sure what my mission was, but I knew I had a destination, a purpose for my hike. Whether that was finding a unique place to sit and think or going somewhere specific, I am unsure. The important part is that I was there in the midst of the lush green hills, enjoying and exploring the captivating creation around me.

The day was turning out to be marvelous. There was not a dark cloud in the sky. I climbed up and down the terrain, maneuvering throughout the trees and rocks effortlessly. Small animals passed by and were not intimidated by my presence. In fact, it was almost as if they enjoyed sharing this glorious day with me. Yes, the day was splendid indeed.

However, as this hike progressed I came to a seemingly endless upward climb of rocks. At first using my hands provided the extra balance I needed to keep climbing. But as the rocks became increasingly further apart, I toiled to find a sturdy place to put my foot. Struggling for quite some time I finally realized I was stuck, and even worse I was not alone. As I looked next to me, I discovered a snake slithering close by and coming to a stop within inches of me. Even though I have a limited knowledge about snakes, I somehow knew this was a particularly aggressive and poisonous snake.

Unsure of what to do I thought if I did not move it would surely leave. On the other hand, if neither of us moved I would be forever stuck there on that hill. Unwilling to compromise my life for the sake of fear, I steadied myself with a deep breath, tried to stay calm, and began to inch away from the snake. My movement must have startled the snake, and it must have felt I had become a threat. Therefore, it did what I had been praying it would not do.

It struck and an extreme pain shot through my leg. I fell to the ground and began holding tightly to my wound. As the venom from the bite began seeping through my veins, I looked around for a way out. I was desperate. How did I get myself into this position? How long could I hold on through the pain of my attack? I wished for a miraculous solution to present itself, but I could not begin to formulate a plan of escape.

Then, in that very moment, I looked up and there it was, my relief. It was him. You know *him,* the adorable, perfect man of whom we all dream. Yes, you know him. He is strong, chivalrous, confident, and masculine; the kind of man we would want to rescue us in our time of despair. He had found me. In one swoop he picked me up, oh how I love his strength. He carried me back to a place of safety where he knew just what to do to tend my wound. In what felt like a moment, I was healed. Not even a scar remained where the fangs had punctured my skin. He knew just what to say to calm my anxious and discouraged heart...oh my sweet, sweet rescuer.

I do not know about you, but my daydream still puts a smile on my face when I think about it. For about five seconds after I had that daydream I got to enjoy the moment. Then the Lord (as He usually does) brought reality back into focus, *His* reality that is. And His reality is this: The story is completely true.

There is journey. We have a destiny, and both are meant to be enjoyed. However, there are rough spots, and unfortunately there is an enemy. And when that enemy sees us taking a step toward freedom, we become his biggest threat. He will strike, and sometimes he will hit. However, remember there is a rescuer, a perfect man of our dreams. He is not some worldly man with limited knowledge, medicine, and resources. He is the MAN of ALL men. He is Jesus—no limitation of knowledge and resources, and He speaks perfect words of love and encouragement. He is our sweet, sweet rescuer, asking you and me today, to *become His beloved.*

How has your Husband been your rescuer? Has there ever been a time when the enemy attacked you? Did you allow your Husband to come in, pick you up, and carry you to safety or did you try to tend to your injury? What words do you need to hear to calm your heart and heal your wounds?

♥

Keeping It Real... Real Personal—Part 1

Day 9

I hope reading these stories has fueled your intimacy with the Lord. And just like the princess walking through dark, foreign places, sometimes we do not feel whose hand we are holding. Life can be difficult, and this devotion came from a journal entry I wrote in one of those hard seasons of learning. However, as He always does, Jesus proved Himself faithful. Let me tell you just how wonderful my Love is. I had been struggling in certain areas of our relationship, namely, trust and obedience to His wise counsel, among many others. For so long in our relationship, I knew He had been pursuing me from the very beginning. God gave me the heart for the ministry, *Becoming Beloved*, years ago, and since then, Jesus has been showing me what it looks like to be His bride and to walk in a close relationship with Him. He had also shown me how He has been pursuing me my whole life. He is so faithful in His pursuit, always reminding me of His unending love and devotion to me. However it was not until this particular time in my life, that He began showing me He had been pursuing me so specifically. Unfortunately though, because of my own stubbornness, I was incapable of being satisfied.

Here I was in this incredible relationship with a perfect spouse, yet I was becoming completely overwhelmed and frustrated with certain situations. Sadly, I would allow my fleshly emotions to override truth, and then the enemy would appear and feast on my weakness, adding fuel to the fire.

The only reason the enemy comes into our lives (if you are a believer) is because we allow him the ground. If you find yourself struggling in your flesh and emotion and begin to feel the enemy's presence, you need to identify the lie you have come to believe. Remember from earlier in the book, if you believed it, then repent. He is faithful to forgive.

Eventually, I snap out of the funk, and I am left looking to Jesus, my Love, asking for His help to heal my hurt (broken, confused, bitter-whatever you feel) heart. Then out of His faithfulness and never-ending supply of grace, He pursues me back to His heart. Many times in my walk with the Lord as His wife, I find myself in hard times like this. This time in particular, I had been in a state where I was hurt and a little broken. So, I sought out one of my best friends and began to weep. Without saying too much, I found her praying freedom from all the lies I had believed. As she prayed, I felt the heaviness lift, and the healing begin. It was there the Lord began to bring revelation. The first thing He showed me was that Jesus is not just a general pursuer. He does not merely pursue me in our general relationship; rather He pursues me to do the things He knows will benefit me. As women, we do not want to be in a relationship with a man who literally walks ten steps ahead with his back turned to us saying "Follow me." We desire someone who walks with us, with his hand on our back guiding us. We want a man who knows the way and has mapped it out for our safety. A man who walks with us, maybe one step ahead, but facing us with his arms outstretched saying, "Come with me." When you are led *and* pursued you get the best of both. This is exactly what Jesus began to show me in that moment. When you are pursued, you are sought after, desired. When you are led, there is a plan. Someone has taken the time to plan the perfect path. You see Jesus not only leads, he leads with pursuit....

What is your pursuer trying to show you through today's devotional? Describe more in detail what it looks like to you, for Jesus to lead with pursuit. How specifically has your Jesus led you in the past? And how specifically do you think He is trying to do lead you in your current situation? What feelings do you need healing from: bitterness, anger, pain? Does the enemy have any ground in your life for attack?

_____

_____

_____

_____

_____

♥

Keeping It Real... Real Personal—Part 2
Day 10

Yesterday's devotion I mentioned God's personal pursuit of us, and how He is not just a general pursuer of us. He identifies areas of our lives where He desires to grow us, then pursues us to fulfill them. Let me give you an example:

For years, I put a certain amount of money into a savings account every month. The amount was nothing astronomical, just a small portion; I planned to use during the first few months after I graduated college. And when the day did come that I graduated, I started to really need that money to pay rent, electricity, water, grocery bills, and other financial responsibilities that hit me all at once. However, at the same time these bills began coming, I really felt I heard the Lord telling me I needed to learn to be a better giver. I was faithful to tithe but had not learned the joy of giving over and above my tithe. I started asking Him, "What am I supposed to give, Lord? I am broke!" Then He pointed to my savings. You can imagine the argument that went on. I just kept asking, "Are you sure Lord?" He kept asking, "Do you trust me, Jenn?" WOW. That was a huge question... do I trust Him? I do not mean do I believe in Him and love Him. Did I trust Him? When I finally decided I had no reason BUT to trust Him, I asked Him one more thing. I said, "God if you are going to call me to be an extravagant giver I need to know that you are going to extravagantly provide for me." I did not mean "Give me all the riches in the world" kind of extravagant. But giving my savings meant saying goodbye to my safety net, and I needed to know He would take care of me.

I was not giving the Lord an ultimatum, "You must do this and say this Lord or else." I simply know that my Love desires to hear me speak, to ask questions, to lean on Him for my help and comfort. So I did. I talked it out with Him. I told Him I really wanted to trust Him, but there was still a little fear in me. Most of this conversation with the Lord actually took place over a few days. During this time, I told no one about this hard decision I was trying to make. He was not even asking me to give away everything, just this one account. Why was it so hard though?

After I had literally cried all my tears and sat in wonderment of the Lord, a sweet friend of mine, who knew nothing of this situation, called me. She told me not to leave my apartment because she was coming over. About 15 minutes later, she knocked on my door, came in and handed me something. She handed me a folded up little treasure, which happened to be the exact amount of money I needed for a bill that was due that week. It was not a large sum of money, but it was the exact amount due for the bill sitting on my counter. God knew my heart was for Him. He knew I desired to be an obedient and trusting daughter, but He also forgave my unbelief and pursued me to trust. He showed me He would provide for all of my needs and showed me that being a giver was more for my benefit than for the people I would bless with my money. He was teaching me faith. He was trying to show me how He longed to pursue me to my spiritual gifting. He led me to my level of ability to trust; He guided me to my obedience. His desire is for me to succeed in what He has called me to do. He will not just ask His beloved to do something. If you open your eyes you will realize He leads and equips His beloved in each thing He desires for her to walk in.

What is He pursuing you to do today? His desire is for you. Will you follow His specific lead and allow Him to pursue you to the great things He has for you? List some areas/ spiritual giftings you know Jesus desires for you to operate in. How is He showing you His faithfulness and equipping you for those callings? Follow Him as He pursues you to become beloved.

_____

_____

_____

_____

_____

♥

He Is No One Night Stand
Day 11

Every time I am in corporate worship nights, I am blessed by seeing God's bride sing love songs to Him. He is so worthy of our praise. In fact, I am often so touched by others worship that I am encouraged to worship Him more. I begin to feel excited, joyful, complete, satisfied; the list goes on.

One night in particular stands out in my memory. I was immersing myself in worship, singing my heart out to the Lord, when something began to stir in me. I felt the Lord trying to quiet me to listen, but I was too busy worshipping! (I know. The irony in that is enough for another discussion in itself.) As worship ended I get into my car ready to drive home. I felt completely satisfied. It was like that great high after a really awesome day. Then I remember the Lord speaking clearly to me. He said, "Jennifer, I am *not* a one night stand." "Excuse me," I thought, "What did you say?" He began to show me that we often get caught up in certain moments with Him and the feelings those moments bring that we forget the relationship He offers. Jesus began to reveal to me that worship to Him was not a cheap, dirty, and scandalous time. It was a sweet, romantic time that came at an extremely high price. Worship to Him is not a cheap fix of joy to live off of for the week. Worship is about preparation of the heart. It is like going on the best, most perfect first date imaginable, as many times as you want, and then realizing the date never has to end. It is a pure, sacred time where we are given the ability to somehow demonstrate to our Love, the gratitude in our hearts for the price of His life.

Now please do not hear me wrongly in this. Those feelings we encounter in worship are beautiful, and they are a gift. There is absolutely nothing wrong with feeling joyful, satisfied, complete, and overwhelmed. In fact, we should have those feelings when worshipping our King. I merely mean to encourage us not to revel in the feelings for the night, then forget what we experienced as soon as the night is over.

Next time you are worshipping remember: Worship does not end.

It is a preparation of the heart to walk in the most beautiful love story ever written. Jesus does not want to romance you and be romanced by you just for the night. He wants to live with you as Husband and have that romance exist between you two all the time. Allow Him to pursue you as you pour your heart out to him, and watch as He continues to show you how to *become beloved.*

When was the last time you really worshipped the Lord? How did you feel as you worshipped Him? Did you continue to worship even after you left the service? Next time you go to a worship service—Allow it to be a time of preparation to hear your Love speak to you. Sometime within the next few days, spend some time in praise in worship (by yourself or corporately) and participate with an attitude of preparation. That part is only the beginning of the romance your Love desires to stir within you.

♥

The Wilderness Part 1
Day 12

Therefore, behold, I will allure her, will bring her into the wilderness, and speak comfort to her. Hosea 2:14

There I was, walking across the stage about to accept my diploma. I reached out and felt the satisfaction of each finger gripping the document, one little piece of paper I had worked so hard during the past four years to obtain. All of the hours and late nights of studying and writing papers all led up to this moment. It was finished. Hallelujah! Now on to a celebration party with my family and friends who had labored in prayer, finances, and words of encouragement over the past four years. Later that evening as I as laid my head down to rest for the day, I recalled the presents, food, fun and accomplishment the day had contained. Oh it was a good day indeed!

Morning after graduation: "Oh my God, Lord what am I going to do for the rest of my life?!" We have all been there, and if you have not, the time is coming. The moment of sheer panic for what the next step should be. Whether that moment came after high school graduation, college graduation, or at the end of a job, we all know the feeling.

While what happens next in the story is not necessarily the norm for every one, this is truly what the next six to eight weeks of my life looked like. I woke up every morning and spent time in the Word, worshipped, prayed, and looked every place I could think of for a job. But I could not find one. I am not even talking about a career. I simply mean a job, something to do to pay the bills. Nothing was panning out.

It was becoming obvious to me that God was trying to teach me something, but to be completely honest I was getting very discouraged. In a matter of one month, every area of my life had changed: I was no longer living next door to all of my best friends; I moved into my own apartment by myself, and I had no job. (The on-campus job I had while in college depended upon me being a student. Now that I graduated, I could no longer hold that position.) This was becoming a difficult season, but I was doing everything I knew to do. I was being obedient to read the Word and pray, and everyday I was seeking a job. I was not just sitting around doing nothing, and although so much was going on spiritually, I still felt alone.

Then one day I had about all I could take. I finally asked the Lord, "What are you doing? I do not understand. Why can I not seem to find a job? Why is it hard to connect with my friends recently?" I remember saying to the Lord, "No matter how I feel, no matter what goes on, or how hard it gets, I will still praise You, Lord." In that moment I felt for the first time in weeks a change in the atmosphere. I remember hearing clearly the Lord speak to me, "Jennifer, did you ever think maybe I just wanted to spend an entire month alone with you?" He said, "I was just waiting for you to speak to me, *really* speak to me. You were so focused on all your issues; you forgot the one in the room with you. I desire your attention. My love, I will take care of you. Just be with Me."

Are you starting to see the overwhelming theme? He desires relationship more than anything else. Describe a time you were in a wilderness, completely confused and not understanding the Lord's purpose. Why do you think He allowed that season? Listen to Him. What is He saying to you right now?

_____

_____

_____

_____

_____

♥

The Wilderness Part 2

Day 13

"And it shall be, in that day," says the Lord, "That you will call Me, 'My Husband,' and no longer call Me, 'My Master.'" Hosea 2:16

Remember the bride's season of wandering before her wedding day described in Section One of the book? A wilderness season is different from a season of wandering. In a season of wandering, you make the decision to leave. The book of Hosea clearly tells us that He allures us and brings us into the wilderness.

Now that I knew my Love had brought me here for a purpose, I began to be more effective in my wilderness. I allowed Him to sing over me His love. Daily, I woke up and asked Him what His agenda was for the day. Without being conscious of Him doing it, He was gently refocusing my gaze on Him. I was not seeing Him as some God I had to do everything perfect for in order to please. It was not about being afraid to make the wrong decision, apply for the wrong job, or live in perfection. He was not some master waiting for me to make a mistake or take the wrong step.

He was my Love, my Husband. A loving husband does not want his wife to be miserable. He does not wait for her to mess up or do something wrong. He desires her to be full of joy in what she is doing. When he truly loves her, he does not want her to come home everyday exhausted and defeated, and he certainly does not want her to live in fear. Quite the opposite, a loving husband will do whatever he can to make sure his wife feels established, happy, and provided for.

Why would God be any different? The answer is, He is not! He literally had to take me to a place by myself for a season in order for me to remember all that He had done for me. His heart was to remind me all that He had promised me from the very beginning.

Don't ask me why the wilderness seasons can be so trying. I wish I knew the answer. While this is how God spoke to me during one of my wilderness seasons, this is certainly not the only wilderness I have been through nor is it the only explanation for such a season. Trust me when I say, I am going to be in the same line with those of you in Heaven wanting to know the answer. We can discuss our theories on the need for difficult wildernesses while we wait for our turn to talk with Job about his trials and tribulations. (Just a thought!)

What wilderness experiences has the Lord been bringing to your mind the past couple of days? Have you ever thanked Him for bringing you through it? Or even for taking you into the wildereness? Take a moment to write your gratitude to your Love for safely guiding you through the wilderness and using it to draw you closer to Him.

♥

The Wilderness Part 3

Day 14

"And now, here's what I'm going to do:
I'm going to start all over again.
I'm taking her back out into the wilderness
where we had our first date, and I'll court her.
I'll give her bouquets of roses.
I'll turn Heartbreak Valley into Acres of Hope.
She'll respond like she did as a young girl,
those days when she was fresh out of Egypt.

"At that time"-this is God's Message still-
"you'll address me , 'Dear husband!'
Never again will you address me,
'My slave-master!'
Hosea 2:14-16 The Message

How beautiful is this translation? He wants to take us back to our first date and court us. He desires to give us bouquets of roses and turn Heartbreak Valley into Acres of Hope. This is too wonderful for me to describe. Take today and ponder on these words. Let today be a day of meditation on His goodness. Even after a woman is married she still desires to be romanced and sought after, and this is exactly what your Husband is trying to show you through this scripture. Read each line and let it move mountains in your heart. Then come back tomorrow to continue on our journey of *becoming beloved.*

_____

_____

_____

♥

YIPPEE! I am so glad you agreed to go on this 14-day adventure with me! Is not our Jesus so sweet? Did you go on a date with Him? Did you attend a worship service? If not, there is still time, make it a priority for your relationship with Jesus. My prayer is during these past two weeks you were encouraged, moved, and challenged to see Jesus in a whole new light. He is not your overseer, hovering over you with a whip to make sure you stay on the straight and narrow, but He is your Love who guides you with grace. Do you see how many precious times with the Lord came straight from my walk with Him? He merely desired for me to look closely at each of the encounters and see Him as the pursuer, rescuer, and romancer of my soul. I think we overcomplicate the idea of walking as His beloved. Being the beloved simply means we understand our identity in Him and His role as Husband and walk in it. (We will discuss identity a little more in the last section.)

Before we end this section and move on to the final one, I want you to notice how several of these experiences easily mirror the story of the wedding day in the first section of the book. This parallel is not coincidental but is because there is still a fleshly side to the relationship. Although we have entered into a marriage relationship with Him, our humanity did not magically disappear. There will be times we fall back into the same cycles of our previous life. But remember Jesus' vow to pursue and love us anyway? He knew we would leave His side occasionally, yet He chose to marry us in spite of our fickle nature. The key is not to attempt to remarry Jesus. Instead, repent and allow the Lord to restart the relationship where you left off. He has a way of restoring stolen time (Joel 2:25).

Thoughts:

_____

_____

_____

_____

_____

♥

Section 4: My Dream Man
Awaiting the Unveiling

It Just Keeps Getting Better

Becoming the bride of Christ is about knowing your identity as His woman. Already in this journey, we have discussed the role of husband and wife and how that relationship correlates to our role with Christ. This final section of the book is meant to prepare us for the unveiling of the earthly marriage.

During the Ketubah study of this book, our hearts were opened and challenged by the question: How are we to know what an earthly marriage is supposed to look like if we ignore the spiritual marriage Christ created for us? My prayer is that we will begin to see He created a broader layout than only the marriage aspect of the relationship. In addition to giving us a beautiful model for marriage, He also gave us a spectacular model for the pursuit. I believe with all my heart that God has been waiting for His children to realize the fullness of what we can have with our future spouse in Him. There is so much we must realize first, however, before we can be ready to actually enter into the covenant of marriage. God greatly desires for us to prepare our hearts to be fully ready for the day He brings us the person He created for us. Part of that preparation for our earthly husband is understanding the season of preparation itself.

While I know there are many incredible books with advice about marriage and engagement, this is not one of them. As the rest of this book has been my heart and personal revelations from the Lord, so is this section. It is simply my convictions and reflections with the Lord that I believe He desired for me to share with you. Much of the material in this final section will seem relevant only to single women. However, I encourage all of you beautiful women reading, regardless of your marital status, to not write off this section as irrelevant. I guarantee if you allow Him, the Lord will speak wonderful things to your spirit during this time.

♥

Being Pursued

This is such a fun part of the journey to go through with you. So much of this process so far has been preparation for these final stages. Several times throughout our journey, we have read the word *pursue*. This word will be an important factor in this next step on our voyage together. Our God is such an intentional God. From the beginning of time, He has been creating in us a unique identity. With purpose, He created us as women to fulfill a place that had not yet been fulfilled in creation. When He created the world He looked and saw that it was good, but then came Adam (Genesis 1:25). In response to seeing Adam, He said, "It is not good for man to be alone" (Genesis 2:18). As a result, he created woman. Therefore, we are an incredible fulfillment in God's creation.

As women, He designed us to react in a particular fashion. With that same intention, He created man to respond in a certain way. I just love the character of our Creator! His perfection in purpose goes beyond our understanding. Until the day we get to meet our Jesus face-to-face, I think there will be questions about why men and women are so different. The only thing we know for sure is that we definitely are different!

There are numerous places to go during this step, but let us start with expanding our knowledge of our role as women. To best do that, we must first understand the role of a man. We have discussed the positions of husband and wife already. This is a more general description of man's role but will really help us as women discover ours. From the beginning, man was created in God's image. Okay, we all understand that! He was created to work. Work for a man was part of God's original plan for him. Often we misunderstand work to be the curse for man, but that is not the case. God created work before the fall of man. Therefore, by nature, men are created to "tend and keep" (Genesis 2:15). From the rib of man and the hand of God, woman was created for the purpose of being a helper for the man. "I will make a helper comparable to him" (Genesis

2:18). He said this after man demonstrated it was not good for man to be alone. "Therefore a man shall leave his father and his mother, and shall cleave unto his wife: and they shall be one flesh" (Genesis 2:24, KJV). When I researched this verse on a man cleaving to his wife, this is what I found: The biblical definition of cleave is to cling, stay close, keep close, stick to, stick with, to pursue closely.[10]

How do these few verses help us understand our purpose in the pursuit? Man was created to do and to work. His role was to care for the things around him. Man was given the ability to take initiative—to see a task that needed finishing and complete it. God realized man should not be alone so he created "a helper comparable," a.k.a. woman (Genesis 2:18). We were created to be his helper and companion. Women were given the blessing to submit, men were given the blessing to lead. The man was called to "leave and cleave." He is called to pursue you. Your role in the course of the pursuit is to be pursued. That is it. I know this is a hard concept for some to grasp, but that is really the truth. As a woman, you are called to be pursued.

However, as women, there is this nasty characteristic that needs to be addressed, and that is the need to control. This need for control is actually what we were cursed with in the garden. A controlling spirit is actually counter-productive to romance. To go to the root of the problem, control usually stems from fear, and we know fear is not of God. Therefore, we must choose to have faith in God's promise and timing. We may rest in His truth and not fear a lack of pursuit or getting hurt. If we are still trying to manipulate the situation, then we are not allowing God to be in control.

Being pursued and waiting on the man to be obedient to God's timing and direction goes against the woman's desire to control, which goes against the blessing God is trying to give her: submission. Again, I pray you understand this. Allow yourself to be pursued. Submit to the Lord; be obedient to Him, and He will bless you with a man willing to pursue you. I am not saying we need to hideout until "Mr. Right" arrives with a ring, but allow the responsibility of initiation and future plans to be submitted to God through your obedience to wait for the pursuit. He is the One who created this idea. Why would He not fulfill His promise and desire for you? That would go against His very nature. So once more, be pursued. Stop trying to manipulate and play games in order to gain the attention of a man. It is your privilege to submit and be sought after.

For some of you, this is very difficult to accept, not because you do not desire to submit, but because you or someone you love has been taken advantage of and mistreated while attempting to be submissive. There is a healing that will need to take place in your heart for you to understand that it is not weakness that calls a woman to submit rather strength and obedience. It was that man's weakness as a leader that is to blame. He was deceived in his belief and understanding of his role to the woman. Forgive him. I know that could be the hardest thing I ask you to do thus far, but it will set you free. Forgiveness frees us. Submission is God's beautiful gift to us as women. Think about it: Why is it easier to understand submitting to God? Christ's love cost Him His life, so it is our joy to honor and submit. If He denies me something I want, I trust it is for my own good. It will be the same with the man God has designed for us. Submission is a blessing when it is God that leads the process. What is the Holy Spirit stirring within you through these words?

_____

_____

_____

_____

_____

♥

Process of Preparation

We have all heard it said, "When you meet him, he will be so worth the wait." However true this statement may be, at some point after hearing this, one of two thoughts have occurred. 1) "Why do we have to wait, and why does it have to be so hard?" 2) "When I do meet him, because of how wonderful he is, I will wish I had met him sooner."

In regards to those two statements, whose best interest are you thinking about? Are you thinking more about him or about yourself? We have all been there at some point and many of us are there now, waiting and praying for our earthly prince to show up. Our patience begins to wear thin, and we are so ready to meet "the one." You need to ask yourself are you really ready? According to 1 Corinthians 13:4, "Love is patient...It is not selfish." Let me ask you again, who are you thinking of when you complain about the wait? I wonder if when you finally meet the guy you will be able to say he was worth waiting for, because the Lord needed to get *me* ready for *him.* Maybe waiting for your earthly prince is your sacrifice for him while God prepares *your* heart.

In order for us to get a better picture, let us take a look at the life of Esther. Esther was a beautiful woman in the Bible who found herself in the midst of many women preparing to be queen. These women entered into a yearlong beautification process in order to come before the king. "Each young woman's turn came to go in to see the [king] after she had completed twelve months' preparation...for thus were appointed six months with oil of myrrh, and six months with perfumes and preparations for beautifying women" (Esther 2:12).

For some reason, when I was planning this book, God kept speaking to me about Esther's season of preparation. He kept showing me how important it is that as women we allow God to put us through the process of preparation. Notice Esther did not have to plan her beauty regiments or even pay for them. Her job was to submit to the preparation. Now, do I think we need to check into a luxury spa for twelve months and be physically pampered and made over? No! Actually, now that I think about it that does not sound too bad! I am kidding. However, I do wonder if we should consider being spiritually pampered and made over.

Maybe we should not necessarily do this for twelve months, but what if we lived in an attitude of being spiritually prepared for our spouse? What if instead of oil of myrrh and perfumes, we prayed for an anointing of purification and preparation that would be a sweet aroma to the Lord and pleasing to our future husband? What if we lived everyday with hearts of purity and patience? Imagine how beautiful we would be to the Lord and our spouse if we practiced the definition of love given to us in 1 Corinthians 13. Is not our first goal to be pleasing to our Jesus so that our spouse will find us while seeking Him? If he is living in a way to model after Christ, then he will look at us as Christ looks at us. For that reason, if we live in an attitude of becoming spiritually prepared, he will find us more beautiful than any earthly model, because he will be looking at our heart. "Man looks at the outward appearance, but God looks at the heart"(1 Samuel 16:7). Therefore, if he is seeking to be like Christ, then he too will look at your heart.

Esther was to live in a state of preparation until her time to see the king. Once she saw him, based upon his delight in her, it was up to him to see her again. However, "she would not go in to see the king again unless the king delighted in her and called for her by name" (Esther 2:14). Once more, we see a representation of the pursuit and direction being the man's decision. She was to be prepared in case the king summoned her.

Ladies, the king will summon you when the timing is right; he will find favor in you. "The king loved Esther more than all the other women, and she obtained grace and favor in his sight" (Esther 2:17). So I ask you what does it look like for you to live in a state of preparation? The man will heed the voice of the Lord and when he is ready he will pursue you. Unfortunately, there is no promise on the timing, but when God appoints the time it will be perfect.

Will you be ready? How sweet is your aroma right now? How fresh is your anointing? Is your attitude going to be a pleasing fragrance to both man and the Lord? If a certain 'king' you have your eye on does not pursue you or 'call you by name' do not be discouraged. God will reward your desire to be obedient to your role. The waiting is hard, but continue to practice love and patience, and you will find yourself fulfilled in the end. If he is worthy of you, he will pursue you. Allow him to lead even before you are married. And if he turns out to not be the one, you will be so glad you waited.

_____

_____

_____

♥

My Dream Man

Now that we understand the joy of pursuit and the beauty of preparation, we can talk about the boy! The fun stuff that since childhood we girls love to get together and talk about. How many slumber parties and girls night out can you remember attending which contained hours of "boy talk" and countless chick flicks? If you are anything like me, the majority of those girl's nights consisted of one major topic...boys.

I remember being at church camp my freshman year in high school listening as my counselor began to give us a task. She handed each girl a piece of paper and told us to entitle it "My Dream Man." On that piece of paper, we were supposed to write down all of the character traits we desired for our future husband. All of the girls sat around giggling as we wrote down the "criteria" for our dream man. After we each wrote down our list of character traits regarding our "dream man," we all shared with each other what we hoped to have one day when we met our prince charming. I remember at the time thinking it was so fun!

Years later when I was preparing to move to college, I came across that piece of paper. As I reread those things I had written years before, I remember beginning to feel a little less hopeful that the kind of man I had dreamed of actually existed. Nonetheless, that piece of paper was packed in one of my boxes and moved with me to college. Then my sophomore year in college, I packed up my things again and moved to a different room. That is when I came across that piece of paper again. Only this time when I read it I thought how unrealistic it was to think that I would find someone like that. I began to feel foolish for wishing such an impossible dream. Later that week, I remember spending some time with the Lord where He spoke something very precious to me. He told me to go back and get that piece of paper and reread it. Here are some of the things I had written down:

- Leader
- Serious
- In tune with God
- Faithful
- Knowledgeable
- Hard worker
- Strong
- Trustworthy
- Self-sacrificing
- Gentleman
- Provider
- Good listener
- Prayer Warrior
- Passionate
- Humble
- Mature
- Obedient
- Honest

In His presence, I reread that piece of paper over and over. I had this sense He was trying to restore the hope in my heart. He *would* give me the desires of my heart (Psalms 37:4). Even in this, He was waiting for me to realize something. Very sweetly, He said to me, "Jennifer can you not see that everything your heart desires can be found in Me?"

That statement warmed my heart. I reread the list again. There it was right in front of me. All I could have asked and imagined was satisfied already in Him. Still part of me questioned Him. "Well, Lord, that is great but what about the other things I desire in an earthly man?" *"What things?"* He asked. I proceeded, "Well I want to find a manly man. You know someone who is not afraid to work with his hands." *"I was a carpenter. I built and worked with my hands"* (Mark 6:3). "I want a man who loves kids." *"I said let the children come to me"* (Matthew 19:14). "A man who is not afraid to cry." *"My word says I wept"* (John 11:35). "A man full of compassion and boldness." *"I stood up to the most powerful forces in government and even when they wrongly accused me, I died for them. I loved you so much that I died for you"* (Mark 15).

- *I was a leader among men and men still follow me today.* Matthew 16:24
- *I lived and dwelt among fallen men, but never once did I sin. I am serious about what I came to do.* Hebrews 4:15
- *I am sitting at the right hand of God; I am in tune with Him.* Hebrews 8:1, John 10:30
- *I will never leave you or forsake you. I am faithfulness.* Deuteronomy 31:6,8

- *I am knowledge and wisdom.* John 1:1, 17:17
- *I set the example for a diligent worker; whatever I put my hands to is accomplished.* Philippians 1:6
- *Even Satan himself could not cause me to give into temptation. That is strength.* Matthew 4:1-11
- *If you trust in Me, I will make your paths straight.* Proverbs 3:5-6
- *I left heaven, dwelt among men, and died a sinner's death for people who would reject me. That is a sacrifice.* Philippians 2:7-8
- *I laid down My life for you, even when you ignored Me. It doesn't get more chivalrous than that.* John 10:11
- *I care even for the birds and the flowers. How much more will I provide for you.* Matthew 6:26-34
- *Pray without ceasing. I love to listen.* 1 Thessalonians 5:17
- *I prayed so hard, My sweat became as blood.* Luke 22:44
- *I am so passionate about you I have numbered the hairs on your head. I know your every heartbeat.* Luke 12:7, Psalms 139:1-18
- *I am the definition of mature, which is to complete or perfect. Not only am I mature, I make you to be also.* Matthew 5:48
- *I humbled Myself and became obedient to death on a cross.* Philippians 2:8
- *I can tell no lie. My character forbids me to be anything other than honest.* Psalms 119:160, Numbers 23:19

Are you beginning to get the picture? Jesus has come to fulfill every longing in our hearts. He is my dream man! No man is fully capable of meeting all our needs. Our wholeness comes not from an earthly man but from Jesus. Everyday I realize this more and more. Often when I tell people this, they begin to think I am against dating and marriage. I promise this is not the case. I am thrilled thinking about the day when God will reveal the man I am going to marry here on earth. However, because of the relationship I have developed with Jesus, I am at peace with the wait.

Now do not get me wrong, it is hard at times to wait, but because every area of my heart is filled with love for Jesus, when He does bring my earthly husband, this man will have to sit on top of the space Jesus occupies. Do you see what happens in this picture? Jesus fills *every* space in my heart. Essentially, He is the foundation. Then when He presents the earthly husband, he will have nowhere to go in my heart, except upon the foundation. Our united relationship will be built on the foundation of our individual relationships with Jesus. Because God will have occupied his heart as well, I will have no place to go in his heart except on the foundation of Jesus. And on this foundation, our house (and marriage) will stand (Matthew 7:24-27).

Jesus does not want me to fall in love with Him and forget about having an earthly marriage. Instead He is trying to show me that when I have given my whole heart to Him first, then I am prepared for His model relationship, a chord of three strands (Ecclesiastes 4:12 NIV). Some of you are still trying to find a formula for the rules of dating and engagement within these pages. I am telling you now, you will not find that here. My goal was not to write a dating and engagement how-to-book. Only the Holy Spirit can speak to you on when, who, and how to date. He works on each of us uniquely in this area because we each have our own weaknesses and temptations. I am going to struggle differently in "this" area than you are and you will struggle differently than your best friend. This is about finding the identity of your heart. You are His wife. That is all you need to know. Your husband is Jesus and that piece of identity settled in your heart will change your perspective on almost everything.

I think it is time for us to finish the story. Remember way back in the beginning of the journey in Section One, when I told you the wedding day story was to be continued? Well, the time has come for us to discover the final scene of that glorious ceremony.

Before moving on, go ahead and write down your list of attributes that you desire in your spouse. Then, take the time to discover in His Word, how He fulfills your heart's desire. Make your list now, do not skip this! It is part of the journey.

To my love: This section made me think of you. I hold no expectation for you except that you hear His voice and follow His lead. I cannot wait to meet you! I love you.

_____

_____

_____

_____

_____

♥

The Wedding Day Continues

I remember my father giving a charge to my love. This was the most significant event throughout the whole ceremony. My father told him, "You are to care for her more than you care for yourself. You will sacrifice everything you have, just so she can wake up and have one more day to be my daughter, to be your wife, to be the woman I have desired for her to be. You are to provide for her, to meet her needs. There are times she will run, there are times she will hurt you, there are times she will not want to be with you. Love her anyway. You will love her with a perfect love, yet she will often forget it. You will often protect her when she does not even realize she needs protection. You will pursue her for the rest of her days. You are to die for her so that she may live."

Not fully able to comprehend everything my father just said, I stood there in awe. Without hesitation, my love said "With pleasure."

Now it was my turn. My father turned to me. Within my father's gaze I see complete joy, peace, and confidence in my decision. With a loving voice he told me, "You, my daughter, honor him. You will be cared for, provided for, unalterably loved. You will often run from this, but your love will always remain, waiting for your return, ready to forgive. You will be protected, desired, found worthy, and pursued all the days of your life. You need only say, 'I do.'"

And because of my father's confidence and the man standing before me, I was able and more than willing to whisper my answer... "I do."

I am overwhelmed. Surely no one has ever felt this happy. Nothing within me can explain the complete feeling of joy and satisfaction that came over me. There was nothing left within my heart to give. Every ounce of me was in love with Jesus. As I look at my Love, Jesus, I cannot explain the feelings being communicated with no words even spoken. We are both overjoyed. He smiles at me as if He still knows something I do not know. He is not smiling like He is being misleading and intentionally withholding information from me. Instead, the look is more a look of anticipation, like He just cannot wait to tell me something. He is looking at the Father then looking back at me. He does this for a moment until the Father gives a nod of approval.

Up until this moment since I stepped up to the altar, Jesus has been standing on my right side with the Father standing in front. The layout is what a typical ceremony placement would look like today. Then as soon as the Father gave His nod to Jesus He does something so strange. Without me ever having to take my eyes off of Him, Jesus steps in front of me and stands directly on the right side of the Father so that I am able to remain focused on both of them.

While Jesus is still holding onto my right hand, He slightly turns my head so that I can see what He was waiting to show me. There on the other side of Him was a man who had been standing there the whole time. An unbelievable peace instantly comes over me. Jesus takes my right hand, which He had been holding, and this man's left hand and joins them. All the while He is still holding both of our hands. Somehow our three hands have become as one. God the Father then places His hand over the set of three hands and breathes His blessing over us. Within that moment, I feel the presence of God (the Holy Spirit) come as a seal and surround this unity.

This man and I have entered into a covenant with Jesus (the model of marriage) as the meeting point, God with His hand of favor and blessing, and the Holy Spirit with His seal of unity. "A chord of three strands is not quickly broken" (Ecclesiastes 4:12 NIV). Within this marriage, there are two sets of three: There is Jesus, this man, and myself. Then there are the three of us, God, and the Holy Spirit.

♥

Do you see how brilliantly orchestrated this event was when He was the one leading it? I, in my human limitation, could not have planned something so intimate and perfect. But notice, Jesus did not show me that there was a man on the other side of Him until I was first fully committed to Him. At first, I believed the sole reason for this timing was to test my commitment. While I do believe this is true, I think there is so much more to His purpose.

He needed me to see that He alone fully satisfies. Even if there was never going to be a man on the other side, I was completely full of life and love with Him. He desired to show me how deep, how wide, and how far His love goes for me. Because of my ability to be fully in love with Him, the man He brought for me is a representation of Christ's desire to come for His bride so that we may have life and have it more abundantly (John 10:10). Our marriage to an earthly husband is merely a blessing. It is a gift we are given by our Love, Father, and Creator. Marriage is meant to be a union with Jesus that is glorified by the Holy Spirit to bring us closer to God. Honor for the Father is meant to be a result of the earthly marriage. What I love so much about the picture of Jesus revealing the earthly husband to me is that I never once had to take my eyes off of Him or the Father. Instead, through the union with my husband and the seal of the Holy Spirit, we were all brought into a closer fellowship.

So about this man who was at the altar... Who is he? Where did come from? How did he get there? What is his story?

♥

The One Worth Waiting For

Did you catch it? Where was the groom while I was walking down the aisle? When I was saying my vows to the Lord? He was there. He was waiting. Again, you see how divine the Lord's plan is for us. Remember earlier when I asked you if your future husband is worth waiting for while God prepares your heart? That is a hard place to arrive at because it requires a death of our own wants and gives life to another's needs. However, when I let myself love a man I have never met (my future spouse) more than myself, God blesses it. By allowing the Lord to become my Husband and prepare my heart, I am enabling myself to be the wife my earthly husband needs.

My earthly husband from the story had to do the same at some point as well. In order for him to be waiting for me at the end of the aisle, he had to go through his own season of patience and preparation. I am curious how hard it must have been for him to be there watching and waiting while I walked through hard times and seasons of wandering. I wonder how much he had to love me to allow me to go through those things so I could be fully satisfied in Jesus. The easy thing for him to do would be to interrupt the process and begin a relationship in his own timing. However, by trusting the Lord and His ways, he allowed me to become the beloved of Christ. He also loved me enough to wait while God worked on his own heart in the areas of trust and patience to make him ready for me.

Now, there is no telling how long your earthly husband has been there before you. It could be a long time or it could be he got to the end of the aisle just moments before you did. The pivotal point is that he is on the same page and in unity with the work the Lord is doing. This is not referring to salvation; remember that is a different moment. The timing of your spouse's salvation is not the issue, but His level of commitment with the Lord is a thing to be considered. What I mean by this statement is that God is not going to lead you to a relationship with a man who does not understand his role as a godly man. God has not been coordinating a love story for you where the man is clueless about his identity to be your husband. One of my favorite parts about the unveiling of the earthly husband is the feeling he had been at the end of the aisle waiting for me. It is like he and Jesus were watching me and talking about how much they loved me while they waited for me.

Sometimes I look back into the vision of that day and wonder if there were times He allowed my husband to leave the altar and meet me certain places in the wilderness. Unknowingly to me, he encouraged me to keep going, to keep running to the end of the aisle to marry my Love. Or, I wonder if Jesus allowed my husband to go and fight battles for me that I did not even know needed to be fought, so that I would get to the aisle faster. I really do not know. Those are just my romantic thoughts coming out. I just know that when I looked into his eyes I knew he had been ready and waiting for me. This part of the story is yet to come for me. I know in my heart what I saw that day, but all I do now is walk completely satisfied in my Love, Jesus, as He continues to prepare me for the physical unveiling of my earthly husband.

Just as I do everyday now, I wonder how often that man is praying for me. I marvel at the amount of patience he has for waiting for me. I get butterflies just thinking about how much I love this man I have never met.

What is the Holy Spirit revealing to you through this segment of our journey? Journal anything new that the Lord is unveiling to you right now.

To my love: I cannot wait to meet you. I look forward to building on top of the foundation of my Love with Jesus a beautiful home of love with you.

_____

_____

_____

_____

_____

♥

Who Is Not Worth Waiting For

So, we are now prepared to let ourselves be led into a beautiful relationship. However, there are just a few things I feel impressed to share with you. There is a difference in being pursued and being chased, as well as being led in a godly manner and being manipulated. Often as women, we see our friends or even find ourselves in an unhealthy relationship, yet we find it so hard to get out of because we want to be patient, forgiving, and loving. This is an incredibly different scenario between a woman in a dating relationship and a woman in a married relationship. I am not married so I will be mainly addressing those in a dating or engaged relationship. Again, God is not going to lead you into a relationship with a man who is selfishly seeking his own desires.

At my current age (mid-twenties), I am watching so many of my friends enter into relationships with incredible men. It is not like they are dating jerks that blatantly treat them like dirt. However, there is a pattern I see of poor timing and good intentions. Many awesome Christian men are ready to enter into a serious relationship and get married. So before praying about it or actually receiving their answer they begin to show interest in a girl. The girl returns the interest, thus, the emotional relationship begins. The next thing you know, the girl is confused because the guy starts withdrawing from the relationship but still flirting when they are together. His answer to her confusion is that he is praying about the timing. This makes absolutely no sense!

I once heard this phrase and thought it was brilliant: "The right guy at the wrong time is still the wrong guy." Here is my personal opinion… and I do mean personal. Take it or leave it; these are just my thoughts. Why would God, who loves you so much, be leading a guy to play with your emotions? Your Jesus does not manipulate and does not tease. If a guy takes interest in you, he should *first* pray about it before making his intentions known to you. Jesus is our defender and our protector and so should the man be for the woman. A man seeking God's heart for your relationship is not going to string you along on a rollercoaster of emotions. He will get his answer from the Lord, and begin his pursuit with God's blessing and direction. Too many amazing Christian men have good intentions in the relationship process but need to be more careful with timing (the if and when to pursue). His intentions should be to guard both of your hearts, not just his own, until the Lord either gives him permission or refusal.

Speaking of good intentions, as women we need to keep close tabs on how far we let our emotions go. We are created to love and be affectionate; hence, caring for a man comes naturally. But we must learn to be more careful with how quickly we give away our hearts. This is the time where scripture becomes very relevant to us when it says to "bring every thought into captivity to the obedience of Christ" (2 Corinthians 10:5). I know it is difficult to wait on the man to pursue or even know if he is interested, but remember it is worth it. Consider the waiting your preparation period. We should not control the man and his obedience to pursue us correctly, but we should control our thoughts and how far we allow ourselves to be emotionally involved.

Remember, it is our choice to say yes to his pursuit. Just because he starts to pursue you does not mean you are obligated to say yes. In the same manner, just because you are in a relationship (outside of marriage) with a man, does not mean you are forced to stay in it. That is what this journey before marriage is about. Not every guy you date is the man you are supposed to marry. Some relationships will be to teach you, and some are entered into out of disobedience. The one true relationship stays the same, our relationship with Jesus. He will always be there. His grace never ends, and just because you are in or have been in a wrong relationship, does not mean God does not already have an incredible man waiting for you at the altar.

When I was writing this section I really felt that some women reading this are in a dating relationship or even engaged and need encouragement to know they have a choice. Do not stay in a relationship out of hope that he will change. Love him enough to let him go in hopes he will find Jesus along the way. Even if he already knows Jesus but this is not the right relationship for you. You are strong enough to walk away. Recall, Jesus is there holding your hand. As hard as it is now, you will be so glad you did, and if it was meant to be, God will restore it in His timing and with His blessing. What is going on in your heart after reading about the one not worth waiting for? Have you ever found yourself in a complicated situation needing an escape? Journal whatever is stirring within your heart right now.

_____

_____

_____

_____

_____

♥

It All Comes Back to Him

We are near the end of our journey together. However, there are few final words I would like to share before I bid you farewell. Even within the process of writing this book, I have met a man who I find attractive. It is such a battle for me to admit these things right here for everyone to read, but I am just like you. I desire to find that special someone. And because has God given me permission to share this with you, then it is my heart for us as women to walk this journey together. Once again, I am going to become even more vulnerable with you. Written below are some of the prayers, journal entries, and encouraging thoughts I find myself pondering on in my current season of life:

Encouraging thoughts:

- "When someone really falls in love with you, you have no competition...Most women define themselves by who loves them. Don't be that woman." –T.D. Jakes
- "You cannot know someone and be closely connected to them without spending any time with them. God, I choose to know you and spend time with you." – Me
- "Honor is foundational truth. If you want blessed finances, you honor your finances."-Russell Evans from Planetshakers Church. *So if we honor our marriage with the Lord, He will honor our relationship in return.*

Prayers straight from my journal:

- "Lord, please help me to take every thought captive and hold it to your obedience. I only want what you have. I have no guilt for having these feelings, because you put this desire within me, but help me to keep my thoughts accountable to you."
- "I don't want to put this man at the end of the altar. I want you to reveal him there. Please protect me from trying to take control."
- "Not an ounce of me gets to pursue; that is me picking up my need to control. I get to say yes and take steps and that is my blessing. Thank you."

Journal Entry:

- Lord, can I be serious with you about my feelings? ~

I love the way he makes me smile. He is so patient. His character challenges me. He makes me smile when he laughs. He is so beautiful. I respect him and have a pure desire to honor him, follow him, and submit to him. He could be my best friend that I fall in love with, but it will take time to get to that place. I love his plans and his dreams. They could so easily be mine. I just want to be around him. I feel like I should feel unworthy to be around him, but somehow, I only feel accepted and comfortable. Because of his quiet confidence and humility, I never have to feel like I need to be anyone other than myself. From the beginning of knowing him, I never pretended to be anyone other than me around him. In fact, he challenges me to be more encouraged about who I am. I could so easily fall in love with him.

I know that is some pretty intense writing, but do you see what God was doing in the midst of that? Even when I became interested in an earthly man, God pointed all my hopes back to Him. Go back and reread that journal entry thinking about Jesus. I am serious, read it again:

I love the way Jesus makes me smile. He is so patient. His character challenges me. He makes me smile when He laughs. Jesus is so beautiful. I respect Him and have a pure desire to honor Him, follow Him, and submit to Him. He could be my best friend that I fall in love with, but it will take time to get to that place. I love His plans and His dreams. They could so easily be mine. I just want to be around Jesus. I feel like I should feel unworthy to be around Him, but somehow, I only feel accepted and comfortable. Because of His quiet confidence and humility, I never have to feel like I need to be anyone other than myself. From the beginning of knowing Jesus I never pretended to be anyone other than me around Him. In fact, He challenges me to be more encouraged about who I am. I could so easily fall in love with Him.

At the time I was writing this I was thinking about a man, but Jesus was showing me when I find the right kind of man, He is still the one glorified. Jesus used this man to show me a physical example of the role He has been dying to fulfill in each one of us. Although nothing will probably come from these feelings, it was *all* worth it just to discover a little bit more of *His* heart for me.

A Day in the Life of the Bride of Christ

Closing Remarks

Well, I hope you have enjoyed this journey with me. The stunning part about this journey is this is merely the beginning. Everyday for the rest of your life, you have the opportunity to wake up and discover more and more what it looks like to be the beloved. Remember your identity as His woman. You are loved, valued, and sought after. I hope you took part in the journey. I truly believe the more you have put into the process the more you are leaving with when you close the book.

I think one of the main points we get to leave with is the fact that being the bride of Christ is about our identity and choosing to walk as His wife. We take every thought captive and remind ourselves who our Husband is! Every moment we spend throughout our day we choose to be His beloved.

When I wake up in the morning, do I look next to me and see Him there awaiting the moment I open my eyes and speak to Him? When I get in the shower is that the time I am renewed and refreshed for a new day with Him? As I eat breakfast, am I reading through His Word for the day being spiritually fed as well as physically? When I walk out the door and get into the car, am I listening as He tells me all of the exciting things He has planned for the day? While I am at work do I listen for His wisdom and guidance for each decision that I make? When something horrible happens at work or in life do I cling to Him to be my comforter, protector, and closest friend? From the moment I walk in the front door after a long day, do I desire to sit down and unload my day with Him? Do I long to spend the evening in His presence speaking and listening to Him? As I lay my head down at night, do I fall asleep talking to Him and telling Him I love Him?

Your identity is an attitude of the heart. God does not desire for you to find yourself in a field afraid, in your torn and dirty wedding dress like the girl from the beginning of the book. Instead, He desires you to be in that same field with Him, clothed in beauty and dancing in freedom. You are the beloved bride. Walk in your true identity my beautiful friend. He is there waiting for you. Walk down the aisle to Him and live as the married bride. *You are becoming beloved.*

Final thoughts, prayers, hopes, truths- journal them now. You are a beautiful bride. Thank you for letting me embark on this journey with you. I love you dear friend.

♥

For Men's Eyes Only

(Just kidding! You can read it too ladies.)

A note for the men brave enough to read this book

Beware of the Pursuer

While preparing to write this book, I promised some of the guy friends in my life I would include a section for them. Well here it goes. There are three things I want to share with you, assuming you have read the rest of the book that is. The first addresses your place as a man. Previously, I briefly discussed your role as the leader and pursuer in the relationship. Be careful of women in your life who desire to pursue you. It seems harmless at first, but it becomes too easy to give in to their pursuit. I understand that it is nice not have to question whether they are interested, but you are a man. Things do not have to be easy. You were created to pursue; women were not.

Control is the root of this desire in women to pursue men. Since that is the case, do you really want what we were cursed with in the garden to be the reason you enter into a relationship with us? I know it sounds a little harsh but it is the truth! The control can be subtle or obvious. Just seek the Lord, and He will reveal it to you. I remember talking to one of my guy friends about this issue. As soon as I was finished talking, he looked at me in shock. He said this was exactly what he had been struggling with in a relationship he was getting in, but he could not exactly put into words what felt wrong about it. For him, it was small things like her always initiating the conversations (texting, email, phones calls, etc.) and times to hang out. For another friend of mine, it was as severe as the girlfriend's need to control the situation and conversation. She would manipulate different scenarios to always make him feel badly if things did not go her way. Whatever it looks like, watch out for the pursuer! You should allow the woman to be pursued. It is not your job to be controlling or manipulative either. No one should have that role in a relationship. You are to lead and pursue her out of her best interest, not your own. Remember her curse is *not* submission.

Her privilege is submission. Therefore, allow her to consider it a joy to submit to you by leading well.

When you give into the control of a woman you are not truly loving her and leading her in your true identity as leader and direction seeker. Believe it or not, you were meant to stop and ask for directions (God's direction on how to lead and pursue!) Something within you will not feel fully satisfied if you are not the one taking initiative and leading the relationship, nor will she be resting in complete peace. Do not lead her anywhere unless you are following direction from the Father. You will only hurt the two of you if you pursue her outside of His timing. Take initiative to seek His will and then be obedient with whatever the answer. I promise it is worth it.

You are the Man!

The second item on my list for you men is this: You are a mighty man of honor. You deserve to be honored and respected. No matter your past, no matter your present, only you and God decide your future. I say only you and God have part in your future because *you* actually do have a part! God has great plans for you (Jeremiah 29:11), but you decide whether you follow His path.

I say all of this because I know some of you have read this book and are currently thinking there is no way I could be a man worthy to be at the end of the aisle waiting for this bride. However, just as the bride in that story at the beginning of the book was made pure and worthy, so are you. You see in God's story, there is no gender to the bride. I used *her* as an example for the purpose of this book, but you are His bride too. Now I know that may sound a little strange, but take it for what it is. God desires for you to become fully committed to Him as well.

Nothing you have done or could do can separate you from His beautiful plan for you and your future spouse (or current spouse for that matter). Understand you are a man of honor. In the Bible, we read about David and all of the sins he committed, including adultery and murder, yet God called him a man after His own heart (1 Samuel 13:14). God loves you and desires for you to be fully confident in your role as a man. You can still be called a man after God's own heart.

Be encouraged today about who you are as a man. I am sorry so much of this perverted world has been deceiving you to believe things about yourself as a man that simply are not true. You are a man called to honor, to be honored, and to live a life of honor. This does not mean you are to be unattached from your feelings or emotions but that you live every area of your life in complete surrender of the one who gave it to you.

I challenge you men to hold every thought captive just as I urged us women (2 Corinthians 10:5). Go ahead and question why you believe certain things about your identity. Hold them up to the standard of man given to you (which is Jesus) and see if those beliefs align according to His truth and identity. You are man; hear you roar!

Romantic at Heart?

Did you know you are a romantic at heart? No really, do not stop reading yet. I am serious. I know these sections are meant to encourage you to be a man and rub some dirt around, but you are romantic. God designed you to be a romantic. He created you after His own image, and He portrays Himself to be the most romantic being that has ever existed. In case you are still not convinced you are going to feel "manly" enough after this section, why don't you read one of the definitions of romantic I found online while researching this word. Go ahead, read it, just below:

Romantic- imbued with or ***dominated*** by idealism, a desire for ***adventure***, chivalry, etc. Synonyms include- extravagant, exaggerated, ***wild***, imaginative, fantastic[11]

And who said it was not manly to be romantic? I know this is an interesting topic for me to choose to write about with such limited space devoted to the guy's section, but I felt it was important. This is just one example where I feel so much of the man's identity (just as the woman's) has been misconstrued by this world. For these reasons, I challenged you before to really ask the Lord what your true identity looks like as a man.

I am obviously not a man, and I am not going to pretend to have insight into your everyday battles and the lies that are thrown your direction. However, I am going to elaborate a little more about the male romantic nature. God is incredibly romantic in every aspect of His pursuit. Why would you not want to be romantic when it gives you permission to be adventurous, to explore the physical world and world of ideas, and to be wild and extravagant?

God purposefully and intentionally made you male. You are created for a purpose: to work and get the job done. He also created you be imaginative, to use your mind on how to pursue and how to fight for what is yours. Just as Jesus pursued and fought for you and me, He created you to do the same for your spouse. That is romantic! Every woman, whether she admits it or not, desires to be fought for and sought after. I hear time after time from women around me, how they do not want to be in a relationship with a man who is not willing to fight for them when things get difficult. Now I know at first this sounds meticulous and could be perceived as another "picky stipulation" women put on men. However the real truth is this is exactly the way God planned it to be!

Does Jesus not fight for you and me every time things get difficult? The frustrating thing is sometimes we are so caught up in our own situation we cannot see Him right there fighting for us. And yes, this happens in the physical as well. You, as a man, could fight with everything within you but because she is focused on her own struggles she may not see it. However, you are only responsible to be obedient and live in the manner Christ desires for you to live. You cannot control the reaction, but you can create an atmosphere for change.

I say all of this to say passivity is a thing of this world. Throw it out. Be assertive in your pursuit and be willing to fight for what God promises you. Just be sure you are seeking His will and His plan and not your own. When you are sure it is His, grab your sword, jump on your horse, and ride! Follow after your promise and watch as you follow God's plan, the enemies He has already fought for you begin to fall (1 Samuel 17:47).

You desire the adventure, the thrill of the chase. You are romantic and trust me, women love romance. That fact will never change. So follow His example, be romantic. Crave the adventure. Be wild. And fight.

Appendix I:
To My Love Worth Waiting For

My love,

I have left you little notes throughout this journey, but this is one note that will only portray part of my heart for you. I love you. I love you. I love you. Words cannot express the depth of my heart for you. I love you so much I am waiting and doing my best to prepare for you. However, when the time does come, please promise to love me despite my flaws. I promise now to love you despite yours. I promise to let you lead me if you promise to let me help you. I am your helper comparable. You are a mighty man of valor. I will honor you. Nothing from your past will hinder me from loving you more and more everyday. I will see the man God has prepared for me, and I will love you. You are so handsome. You leave me breathless when I think about you. I have such a desire to follow wherever you lead me. I trust you because I trust Him. I cannot wait to meet you, my best friend, and grow old with you. I want to laugh with you and see the world with you. I cannot wait to be challenged by you and encouraged by Jesus within you. I know you are waiting there at the end of the aisle. Just keep waiting... I am coming. I promise.

With all my love,

~Yours

Appendix II:
Salvation Prayer

Lord Jesus,

I confess that I am a sinner. Thank you for dying on the cross for my sins so that I might have a relationship with you. Please forgive me of my sins. I turn from my old ways of wandering and sin and choose to follow as you lead me as My Lord, Savior, and Love of my life.

Amen

Next Step:
You did it! Congratulations! You are now a member of the body of Christ and get to walk in a close relationship with Him. This is the best decision you have and will ever make! I encourage you now to find a fellow believer and tell them about your decision. Also, find a local church that can give you the help in beginning your journey of being a Christian. I love you dear sister (or brother) and I am rejoicing with the rest of Heaven in your decision!

Notes

All Scripture is taken from the NEW KING JAMES VERSION of the Bible unless otherwise noted. Copyright © 1982. Thomas Nelson, Inc. Publishers. Printed in the United States of America.

All other Scripture translations, other then NKJV, were used from Bible Gateway.com. 2011. http://www.biblegateway.com.

Section 2 Notes:
Dictionary.com. Accessed June 20, 2011. http://dictionary.reference. com/browse/condemnation.
Shulman, Chaplain Shlomo. "Guide to the Jewish Wedding." Accessed June 21, 2011. http://www.aish.com/jl/l/m/48969841.html.
Lamm, Rabbi Maurice. "The Ketubah Text." Accessed June 21, 201. http://www.myjewishlearning.com/life/Life_Events/Weddings/ Liturgy_Ritual_and_Custom/Ketubah/Details_I.shtml.
Lamm, Rabbi Maurice and Shulman, Chaplain Sholomo. See previous endnotes.
Dictionary.com. Accessed June 22, 2011. http://dictionary.reference. com/browse/support.

Section 3 Notes:
Dictionary.com. Accessed June 20, 2011. http://dictionary.reference. com/browse/virtue.
Dictionary.com. Accessed June 20, 2011. http://dictionary.reference. com/browse/merely.
Dictionary.com. Accessed June 20, 2011. http://dictionary.reference. com/browse/quiet.

Dictionary.com. Accessed June 20, 2011. http://dictionary.reference. com/browse/gentle.

Section 4 Notes:

Blue Letter Bible. "Dictionary and Word Search for *dabaq (Strong's 1692)*". Blue Letter Bible. 1996-2011. Accessed June 19, 2011. http://www.blueletterbible.org/lang/lexicon/lexicon.cfm? Strongs=H1692&t=KJV.

For Men's Eyes Only Notes:

Dictionary.com. Accessed on June 26, 2011. http://dictionary.reference. com/browse/romantic.

About the Author

Jennifer K Davis is the founder of Becoming Beloved Ministries. She has a tremendous passion for sharing the truth that all are the bride of Christ. Her heart is for every woman, no matter their stage of life, to be able to have an intimate relationship with Christ. Jennifer currently resides in Irving, Texas and is a member of Gateway Church.

Becoming Beloved Ministries

Becoming Beloved Ministries is a non-denominational ministry desiring to deepen the relationship of Jesus with His bride. We are focused on bringing Truth to the identity of every woman that she is loved and found worthy in the eyes of her Savior. Our passion is to awaken the heart of women to be fulfilled by the true Love of their life, Jesus Christ.

For more information visit www.becomingbeloved.com

CPSIA information can be obtained at www.ICGtesting.com
Printed in the USA
LVOW070059291011

252577LV00001B/4/P